Foxeartl

The History of an East Anglian Brewery

by Richard Morris

Foxearth Brew

The History of an East Anglian Brewery

by Richard Morris

First published 2004 by the Foxearth District History Society
Orchard House Foxearth CO10 7JG
www.foxearth.org.uk

"Evidently, from several staggering forms observed in the church and the churchyard in the evening, not only St Michael, but also Bacchus had been commemorated" The Bury & Norwich Post, October 10th.1863; describing the celebrations for the restoration of Foxearth Church

Copyright Richard Morris 2004

ISBN 0-9548193-0-6

For information on the Foxearth & District History Society, including

Bygone newspaper stories and photographs log on to:

www.foxearth.org.uk

Typeset by Andrew Clarke

CONTENTS

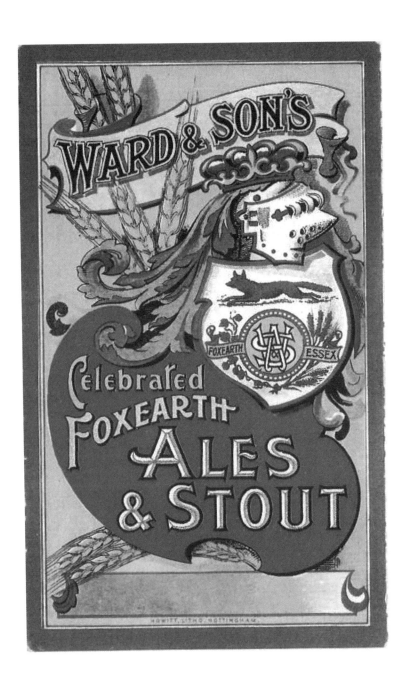

WARD & SON'S

Celebrated FOXEARTH ALES & STOUT

FOXEARTH ESSEX

HOWITT, LITHO, NOTTINGHAM.

INTRODUCTION

Until I started writing this book, I had little idea of what a 'biography' of the brewery involved; not for the reader, but for the writer. Rummaging in private letters and wills, reading things that until then, few others had read, so the point comes where the writer knows scarcely less about a family than its surviving members do. It is a big intrusion.

If this is an intrusion, think how much more of one it is when something unexpectedly crops up, as it did in this case. Then it is like opening a door, slightly nervous of what you might find, for these were secrets that were never intended to be spoken about.

It is scarcely two lifetimes ago since founders of the brewery, George and Charlotte Ward, first set up as brewers in the late 1840s. We know that George was born into an agricultural family that had settled in Foxearth at least three hundred years before his birth and that his future wife Charlotte (nee Miller) was born at Walsham Le Willows in Suffolk, but that is really all we know about them. Records that were in the brewery lofts and carelessly discarded by Charrington's in the 1980s may have helped, of course.

Whether George or Charlotte decided on the idea of making money from brewing we shall probably never know but what is clear is that the business grew far more rapidly in years after George's death than when he was alive; though improved communication and transport had a good deal to do with the brewery's growth, the greater reasons behind the success will be revealed as one reads this book.

Much more is known about their enterprising son David Ward - and what a remarkable entrepreneur he was. From his early days in charge of the brewery's development to the last, in which, in old age and beyond what would be the care of most, he was enjoying himself directing a business that was to achieve more awards than any other brewery of any size of any country in Europe.

Perfection was his ideology and enterprise his instinct; much of the money the company made was invested back into buying new machinery and taking advantage of the best that brewing science had to offer. He was also altruistic. As well as introducing running water to the village he gave it electricity; the village hall; increased leisure facilities and employment.

His firm, Ward and Son was a company of firsts. Throughout its early life, it was not just a year or two ahead of its time but at least a decade. It was one of the first in the UK to cold-filter its beers in 1881 and it was close behind the huge firm of Whitbread's in bottling its beer.

By 1931, it was producing over 20,000 barrels of beer annually and 12,000 bottles of beer a day.

The firm was later sold at a time when fierce competition was being made by the large breweries into the independent trade and although a reverse takeover was set up a short time afterwards, Ward's never brewed beer again after 1958. The company was hived off to Charrington United Breweries Ltd in the early 1960s and served as a radial supply depot and warehouse until 1987.

Sadly, there is little to see of the business that once gave a dependent living to so many people down the years. The office buildings and engine house remain, but the great three-storey brew house, ancillary buildings and 75-foot high chimneystack were demolished a generation ago; a housing estate built in their place - though thankfully, the brewery's legacy and testimony to its success cannot be so easily wiped away.

Everybody who has either read or written a biography will know that – with certain epic and heroic exceptions – the number of vivid and active years in any given life are depressingly and remarkably few. As there is still much material in private hands, (nowhere have I been able to find the 1919 Ward's Limited prospectus) the following necessarily offers an account of the people that once worked and shaped the village's economy and social landscape; the people that shared the lawful limelight and who made this remarkable business work. I have tried to represent past events as best as I can and would be delighted to hear from anyone who thinks that I may have left something out that should have been included.

Richard Morris, Foxearth 2004

Aerial view of the brewery in the late 1950s

FOREWORD

How lucky we are that Richard Morris has used his journalistic expertise to provide us with such a refreshing slant on local history.

His 'biography of a brewery' vividly illuminates the village of Foxearth as it was, together with life and social conditions along the Suffolk-Essex border from 1840-1960.

Yet we are treated to more. We follow the birth, phenomenal growth and eventual demise of a business enterprise; we see the effect of twentieth century change on both that enterprise and the surrounding community and we share in the heartache and loss of the First World War.

This is a local history – but one that is placed in a regional and national context. As we turn the pages we feel we are living through bygone decades; we smell the malt and hops in our nostrils and we come to know the personalities involved, until finally, at the end, we feel sadness at the brewery's closure.

I am delighted to commend this book.

Ashley Cooper
President, Foxearth & District Local History Society
Gestingthorpe 2004

Note that additional pictures and other supplementary materials about the Foxearth Brewery are available at the Foxearth & District Local History Society's website at www.foxearth.org.uk

PASTURES NEW

Brewing in mid-Victorian rural areas demanded rigid self-sufficiency with materials close at hand. In prime barley growing areas malt was easy to come by; yeast, that vital seed, was irresistibly passed from house to house and villagers regularly set aside land for hop cultivation, though it was nothing compared to the glory days of the 1760s when Essex was considered a serious hop growing rival to Kent and Sussex. In the mid 1800s, Foxearth had three acres set aside for growing hops, which yielded close to fourteen hundredweight for brewing purposes.

The majority of the harvest would have been sold to a merchant with some kept back for brewing locally by people such as Joseph Theobald, who in 1845, is recorded as Foxearth's first beer retailer.

Doubtless he had taken advantage of the 1830 Beerhouse Act, which had been set down 15 years earlier by the Duke of Wellington's government, ostensibly to help the poor and to liberate an industry by allowing better competition. To all intents and purposes, almost anyone wishing to sell beer could do so by paying two guineas to the Excise. Not surprisingly many of these 'free-houses' in villages became haunts of criminals and helped to peddle adulterated beer, sometimes laced with all sorts of narcotics such as Deadly Nightshade and Sulphur. Though penalties for brewing with anything other than malt and hops were severe, the prosecution of brewers was heavily reliant[1] on people able to detect different substances in the beer; but the Act did realise its original purpose by creating a free-market.

Almost 40,000 beerhouses[2] were in business within ten years of the Act being passed with the vast majority outside London – the Act was eventually repealed in 1869, when magistrates were again responsible for issuing licences.

---

[1] Newspapers of the day regularly reported Excise men closing down breweries and destroying brewing equipment.

[2] From A History of Beer & Brewing by Ian Hornsey published by RSC Paperbacks

The simple way in which pre-1869 licences had been handed out, saw the proliferation of beerhouses in nearby villages; two served Borley; Glemsford had three, Pentlow one; Belchamp St Paul's made do with three and Foxearth had two up to 1868 when one was mysteriously burnt down following a quarrel over a neighbour's cat.

To make matters worse, the village had lost its solitary alehouse in the late 1840s when The Fox public house had been demolished to make way for a school. An adjunction to the *History of Essex*, published May 1852, describes the theory behind the demolition:

"The schools occupy the site of the village alehouse, which the Rector [John Foster] purchased, with the double object of appropriating it to the beneficial purposes of education, as well as removing the source of idleness and intemperance."

Hedonism was a marked feature of labouring life in agricultural districts and the village alehouse was usually the only meeting place for workers; unfortunately, these assemblies were often looked on by landowners according to London's Pall Mall Times nests of agitation where: '...*evil is hatched, and from there men take their first journey on the road that leads to gaol. The place is often crowded at night - there is scarcely room to stand, the atmosphere is thick with smoke, and hoarse jarring of voices fills it, above which raises the stave of a song, shouted in one unvarying key or another from some corner.*'

The remaining beerhouse in the village was The Lion, located in The Street, the main road in Foxearth where the brewery offices were later built. Joseph Theobald ran the off-licence for three years before selling the business to one Elisha Deal.

When she retired in 1855, The Lion was to go to auction at Sudbury that September, however before the property had a chance to go public, the village Rector, the Rev John Foster who just three years earlier had demolished the ale house, bought The Lion by private treaty and installed 'by earnest recommendation' a brewer that was making a name for himself called George Ward. White's Gazetteer for 1848 identifies Ward as a maltster and brewer who was carrying out his trade at the Windmill in Mill Lane, Foxearth, where Elisha Deal was the Miller. Bearing in mind that most villages around the Stour had a mill, it was usual to find beer being brewed for workers and the surplus sold. In the late 1840s Ward was delivering beer by horse and cart in 1 gallon and 2 gallon stone casks to inn-keepers at Cavendish and Sudbury.

The same auction, which took place at the Rose and Crown Hotel in Sudbury, refers to a house called The Cottage[3] with an estate of about 2 acres which was later to become one of three large houses David Ward and subsequent generations of his family would make their home. The Cottage had been used as a boarding school up until 1852 by a Miss Ince and part of the contents of her estate included a malting office measuring '12 coombs deep' (a coomb was a 16 stone sack of malt and measured 8ft 6in in length) a brew house, a granary as well a small carpenter's shop tenanted by Dominic Branwhite. [4]

Foster bought the estate and house and installed his son, John Francis, who was curate at the parish church. The brewhouse, a common feature of the time in rural districts, was given over to George Ward. Foster senior, who had amassed a fortune from his grandparents and augmented it through judicious marriages, is likely to have bought The Lion for several reasons but besides the obvious ones: beer being a heavily lucrative trade made for a good investment and of course the Rector could choose who he leased the shop to; The Lion sign was often adopted by landlords in derision of the Puritans or dissenters, who showered biblical phrases whenever they could possibly do so. It may be a coincidence of course, but during this decade the village's Congregational scene was one of triumphant militancy.

George Ward was the first generation of his family to become a 'common' licensed brewer and maltster. Originally, from an agricultural background, he was born at Western End, Foxearth in 1814, eldest of five children to Samuel and Martha Ward (nee Mortlock) who was born at nearby Cavendish.

---

[3] Now called Hunters Lodge

[4] His son Wesney later built a maltings in Long Melford called Branwhites. The maltings has been largely rebuilt in a sympathetic manner and turned into flats. The only original part of the maltings to have survived is a building abutting Station Road.

Like his father before him, he was an agricultural labourer, first at Foxearth Hall, then Claypits Farm in the village where he graduated to farm bailiff. It was while he was at the Hall that he won first prize at the prestigious South Suffolk Agricultural Show in 1839 for foot-plough work.

Around the late 1840s, George met and amused a girl named Charlotte Miller, a miller's daughter from Walsham le Willows in Suffolk. In 1850 they married at Foxearth parish church (rural Victorian courtships were rarely long spun out affairs)[5] with people turning out in force to solemnize the wedding of a well-known son. One of the two witnesses to the marriage was William Christmas, owner of a small craft brewery near Haverhill and husband to George's sister Mary. A generation on, and their son Frederick bought the Haverhill Brewery in Camps Road in 1894 from William Ward & Son, distant cousins to David; a nice convoluted family connection.

In 1855, when the Ward's together with their 4-year-old daughter Amelia decided to accept the Rector's business proposition and supplement their brewing business, they knew that hard work pervaded and influenced everything they did and certainly George must have had great confidence in his craft to take such a gamble.

What may have helped him turn away from agriculture, was that right through the mid 1800s the home brewing of ale and beer was declining fast - the high prices of raw materials and the taxes imposed as a result of the Napoleonic wars had made it expensive. Nevertheless, beer was still the usual drink in most households for both adults and children; tea was drunk as well but the tea-drinking habit was largely the reserve of the rich as it was much too expensive for an ordinary family.

In his seminal book on English village life in the small East Suffolk village of Blaxhall, the English folklorist George Ewart Evans who wrote *Ask the Fellows Who Cut the Hay* gives a classic

---

[5] Some of the rituals of courtship were open to misunderstanding from outside the community. Not least of these, was the widespread practice of delaying marriage until the girl was pregnant; it relieved young couples of the hardships of setting up home for as long as possible and also confirmed the woman's child-bearing ability.

description of how beer was made in rural households. It would be a heady brew, like a porter, a characteristically dark brown beer, the bitterness of which derives from the use of roasted, un-malted barley. It is worth quoting in full, if only to understand what a laborious process brewing could be:

The utensils used in the brewing were, with one exception, made of wood. They were: a brewing tub or keeler, made of wood and banded with iron, for steeping and mashing the malt; an under deck, another large wooden tub; a faucet and taps; a beer-stool or wooden stand for holding the barrels; a horsehair sieve for straining sometimes called the hop-sieve from its use in holding the small hop-seeds and preventing them from entering the finished beer; a rack or tongs on which the sieve rested during the straining process; a funnel for pouring the beer in the casks; a hand-cup or jet, a scooped out wooden ladle; a wilch (wilsh), a bottle shaped piece of wicker which was used to filter the liquid or wort from the mash of steeped malt and a six or ten pail copper, which would be a fixture in the house not far from the brick-oven.

The ingredients for a small brew were: one bushel of malt; one pound of hops, and a pint of yeast.

After lighting the fire under the copper, the brewer (usually the woman in the household), set the brewing tub on the stool and placed the wilch over the tap on the inside of the tub. Then six pails of cold water went in followed by three pails of boiling water. Into the water went the malt - on the side of the tub away from the tap.

The brewer then drew the malt from one side of the tub to the other. This was done until every kernel was wet. To get the malt grain out of the wilch and to enable the wort to run freely, the tap was opened and a bucket of the liquid was drawn off which was then poured back into the tub. Then another bucket of hot water was used to rinse round the top of the tub and the wilch to ensure that not one particle of malt was left dry otherwise the brew would be spoilt.

A rack was placed over the tub and covered with a cloth and sacks to keep in the spirit of the malt. The steeped malt was then left for fifteen minutes.

Five pails of boiling water were taken out of the copper and poured onto the malt. The resulting mash was stirred for about ten minutes; covered up and allowed to stand for four hours - no longer. The wilch was then cleared in the same manner as before. All the liquid or wort would then be drawn off into the under deck which as the name implies would be a lower level than the keeler.

There would be five or six pails of wort in the underdeck after this process.

In the meantime, the copper had been filled with four pails of water. When this water boiled it was poured onto the mash left in the tub to make the second wort. The second wort stood for four hours as did the first.

The first wort was then taken from the underdeck, poured into the copper and three quarters of a pound of hops were added to it. This was boiled up with the hops until the second wort was ready to be drained off. The first wort was then drained through the hair-sieve into the underdeck. The second wort was drained off from the mash and then boiled in the copper for four hours, exactly as the first wort. The hops were used for a second time with quarter of a pound of unused hops added to it. Before the hops had been added to the wort this was known here as 'sweet watt' and was much sought after by the children who would be just allowed to taste it.

After the wilch had been taken out of the brewing tub, also the remaining drains of malt, the second wort was then strained off into it to cool. The second wort gave small or mild beer; the first wort - if kept separate - strong beer. But in many places the two worts were mixed together to give nine or ten pails - about twenty gallons - of beer.

One pint of yeast was added to the beer when it was milk-warm. A couple of clean corks, or a slice of toasted bread, were placed on top of the beer; the yeast was poured in and as it began to work it collected around the corks. When this process began and the pleasant sight of the mushroom of yeast starting to form around the corks, the brewer knew that the beer could be left to itself.[6]

The next morning the yeast was strained off and the beer put into casks. These were left uncorked, and by the next day, a little yeast would have worked out of the bunghole. The remainder of the yeast was carefully skimmed off and the same process repeated for three or four days. The casks were then bunged down.

The beer was left at least a week before being drunk; although people who liked young beer often tapped the casks before the lapse of this period. As a variation on the above process, some brewers reserved three or four pails of the first wort and placed two handfuls of clean wheat into the cask with the beer. This would keep for a year, as all the time the beer would be feeding off the wheat.

The process sounds magical, romantic, and to modern eyes, accustomed by the exquisite but discriminating watercolours of Helen Allingham or Birket Foster, and by the romantic recreations of period films, the Victorian village looks an idyllic place. No cars, no fertilisers, homemade food and drink, none of the stresses and strains of modern life: all is picturesque and appealing.

In fact both the Victorian urban and suburban middle classes were so enamoured with Helen Allingham's 'lovely little transcripts' of everyday life and pleasantly prettified village sketches of Mary Russell Mitford that they were never out of print, with the Victorians warming to Mitford's 'busy, merry, stirring little world' which offered no reassurance to those living in desperate poverty.

One of the more hard-headed of the social explorers, G.F. Millan, a journalist and special correspondent for the *Liberal Daily News*, has left one of the most evocative pictures of that idyll-that-never-was. In his description of a village in Suffolk bordering on Essex he paints a delicious but flawed scene:

Here is a vicarage garden with a party at lawn tennis; yonder through that woody vista is a small company of harvesters;

---

[6] Housewives sometimes practised the ancient method of preserving yeast by dipping handfuls of birch twigs in liquid yeast, hanging them up to dry and keeping them for the next brewing session, when one of these small brooms was thrown into the wort. It was then extracted and used for the next brew.

now you have a rosy looking woman shaking down the plums
for a fair-haired child. Peace and quiet, beauty and
fruitfulness, prevail everywhere.

The longing of the sophisticated for a simple life, and of the urbanised for a rural one, had already taken hold. Against such a strong mental image of peace, contentment, healthy hard work and honest fare, no evidence to the Royal Commission about the grinding poverty of the countryside could make much headway.

Although the bulk of the rural population was very poor - their average weekly cash wage in 1851 was nine shillings and seven pence - their lives were made supposedly more bearable by farmers improving workers various privileges by upping beer and 'nutrients' allowances to two quarts (four pints) a week. The claim was essentially true if slightly evasive. Beer was often looked on as an all-round food, never mind that it offered small comfort from its slim scope of minerals and vitamins.

Employers often blatantly manipulated the working lives of their employees; defiance meant dismissal and there was nothing particularly attractive or stimulating about rural life. Pleasures and recreations were very few and drunkenness was endemic, but this has to be understood in the context of the general impoverishment of any social life. It required relentless effort just to be able to pay the rent let alone feed oneself and a family.

As the splendidly named G.J. Monson-Fitzjohn, a correspondent writing for the *Illustrated London News*, noted of the villages of Suffolk and north Essex:

"Drunkenness in these remote hamlets is a recreation for
those whom it has become habitual. Hard workers have little
else to attract them and regularly go on periodical drinking
sprees even though they are scarcely able to afford to bring
home enough money with which buy bread with. It gives great
riches to the brewer of beer. If it is good beer then so much
more is his wealth."

Western End Foxearth.

100313

Western End where George Ward was born in 1814

THE WIDOW AND THE LION

By the time of his early death at the age of 64 in 1878, few in the area could rival George Ward's skilful brewing. His business had afforded him to school all his children privately and convinced George's widow that she and her 19-year-old son David should continue to live at The Lion and trade as Mrs Charlotte Ward & Son. As well as taking over the brewing and the running of the beerhouse, Charlotte continued to act as an agent for Greene & Son's 'celebrated ales and stout'- the company founded by the Bury St Edmund's brewer and which would later become Greene King. [7]

Life for Charlotte was undoubtedly hard. She had not been brought up in a protective cocoon like her middle and upper class counterparts and keeping a beer house was no easy task for a woman, especially as many men disapproved of women earning at all as they believed work and wages de-feminized the gentle sex. Such a view totally discounted the immense courage and strength of character, which women brought to their dual tasks as wage earners and housewives. It must have been a miserably sad and lonely time for her.

The Lion was very much a male preserve and although it had only an off-licence, newspaper stories of the time have reports of 'drunken garden frolics' at the rear of the relatively respectable shop so obviously beer was being enjoyed on the premises. Of course many men who went out for the evening merely nursed a pint for duration; chronic overindulgence was beyond the means of most but

---

[7] Although Amelia had moved out of her parent's house she was still living in Foxearth and near to her family. In the previous three years she had trained as a teacher and was now working at the village school. Her father's memory lived on, through his business and through the Redwood tree he had planted in the Rectory grounds in the 1860s. The Redwood was destroyed by lightning in 1987. A replacement was planted by George's grandson, Harold Ward, later that year.

for those who did, with mournful irony, get as drunk as Lords and lose themselves in a daze of drink it could lead to the poor-house. In a comic but poignant letter dated 1881, a Foxearth resident, Mrs Eady, wrote to the Sudbury Board of Guardians[8] asking for their advice as she feared ending up in the workhouse if her husband could not curb his sporadic drinking spells.

> *'Everybody in the village knows my husband is a hard working man and everyone knows when he has had a drinking bout helped by Ward's beer for he proclaims the fact wherever he goes, and tells whole gatherings again and again about how much he can drink. He thinks he has a perfect right to do as he pleases without anyone telling him otherways. Please help me to give him what for.'*

For women there was little to alleviate the ensuing gloom and no respite from family cares except for the exchange of tittle-tattle, which Richard Jeffries, a social commentator in the mid-1870s unkindly characterised as their 'chief intellectual amusement' Not surprisingly The Lion provided an important social function and here the small minutiae of village life would be alluded to with the same thoroughness as the leasing of a harvest field, until not a grain of interest or novelty was left.

In the evenings, sitting in the rear garden over their mugs and tankards of beer, smoking their short clays and talking might be numbers of men, mostly agricultural workers where dull days broke out into life with interchange of talk, snatches of folk songs, and some show of fun. Some men would have spoken in what was called the dubitative or approximating style. The farm labourer for example, would be feeling for what he had to say through a maze of tangled expletives, qualifications, retractions, and corrections. He would have known that he was unsure of his ground, that he had not said what he had in his mind and would be afraid of the consequences of articulate speech, but expected to gain nothing by

---

[8] The Foxearth Workhouse in Mill Lane was sold in 1834. The poor now became the responsibility of the Board of Guardians. Rev John Foster was for many years Chairman of the Sudbury Board of Guardians (1856-1883) which was situated where Walnut Tree Hospital now stands in Sudbury. David Ward later served on the Guardians Board as an 'ordinary committee-man'.

silence, however a sense of superiority of one's own community was sustained by the repetition of traditional jests and taunts celebrating the supposed failures of one's nearest neighbours.

The importance of folk song to the rural community was very high for it supplied the village with a fund of narrative, humour and social comment in a language everybody could understand and a mode in which everyone could participate. It was simplistic but it had to be.

The men could all join in 'companionship singing'. The companionship was intensely local with many families joining together to draw out memories and tell musical stories – particularly ones involving ghosts and magic.

The legend of the Borley haunting has more than a touch of storytelling brilliance behind it. The well-known story is that a young monk fell in love with a beautiful young novice from a nearby nunnery and they would meet in the nearby woods. After some time they eloped in a black coach drawn by a pair of horses and driven by another lay brother. The couple were soon missed and tracked down; the would-be bridegroom was later lynched and the nun bricked up alive. A moral tale if there ever was one.

But drink also had its curses; without doubt, those families where the husband was a teetotaller were both financially stable and emotionally better off, for drink then as now, offered excitable temperaments an outlet for violence. One social commentator said it was a wonder that Britain was a great empire with men he considered not men but *members of a vast seedy, over-worked, over-legislated, neuter class, with their drab clothes, their un-envious, stricken living conditions, old-world apathies and resentments. No wonder they loose their sensibilities and rationality through drink.'*

John Maldon's interview with a labourer for the London Evening News in 1874 illustrates how a good man was being driven to violence by drink and despair:

"She asked I for money, she did, and what was I to gi'eher? I hadn't got a sixpence nor a shilling, and she knew it and knowed that I couldn't get one either till Saturday night. I got to buy victuals with money, let alone beer. And a man can't do no work wi'out a quart a day, and that's near four pence, that's my share, look 'ee, gone at onst. I know I drinks beer,

and more so than I should. It makes me kinder stupid, as I don't feel nothing then. Wot's the good - I've worked this thirty year or more, since I wuz big enough to go with the plough, and I've knowed they as worked for nigh handy sixty, and wot do 'em get for it? All he'd a got wuz the rheumatiz. Yer med as well drink wile 'ee can. I never meaned to hurt her, and her knows it; and if it wurn't for a parcel of women a-shoving her on, her would never have a come here agen me. I know I drinks, and what else I be to do? I can't work allus."

The work of running the beershop would certainly have helped to relieve Charlotte of some of the burdens of care and caused at least some ambivalent regard to the future. Only a year previous to George dying, her sister had died prematurely but it was a little early in her life for the years of regular obituary and funerals, in any case, true to her age and upbringing, she would have seen it as her duty to adapt. There was still time to make plans for the future. Turning a cottage industry into a thriving business required equal amounts of vision and capital. Without any doubt, Charlotte was an achieving, enterprising woman even though she had the burden of running a business, making a home and looking after her son David, and this before the days of electricity, running water and labour-saving devices was backbreaking work.

In addition, food and clothing had to be provided and the way in which cottage women managed to make do won the admiration of all who observed it especially people who studied the welfare of villagers such as John Foster. This connection was destined to prove critical in the future financing of the Ward's business.

During his lifetime Foster was a figure of considerable controversy. Nor did controversy cease with his death. On the one hand, he was identified as a savant, helping to encourage small triumphs for his parishioners such as offering education to their children. He took to help any member of the parish who he felt was being unfairly treated or who was in any difficulties. On the other hand, Foster enforced a feeling of disloyalty amongst those who he was there to serve and seemed to abandon his calling. No more so than on 12 December 1871, when he was arrested for allegedly raping a 16-year-old Foxearth girl named Sarah Newman. Being guilty of rape carried the capital sentence and he knew no mercy was likely for a man in Holy Orders. However, at his pre-trial hearing the power of the Vestry showed and he had his luck with magistrates who refused to commit the case to a higher court.

The Bench at the Petty Sessions at Castle Hedingham[9] heard the Rector's solicitor make much of his client's problems with two landowners named Simon Quy Viall and Edward Gardiner. What had started as a dispute over land had turned into something of a vendetta. The whole episode had been hatched by three closely linked families and it was this that had led to the court appearance and allegations, argued his counsel. Oh, and the Newman family did not report the crime straight away, instead they waited nine months to do so.

After several hours of lobbying and close questioning of young Sarah, the Bench dismissed her allegations and Foster was acquitted. But even the pre-trial was not without incident, when it was rumoured that the girl's father, a principal witness in the case, had been stopped by a stranger who had bought him drinks in several public houses on the way. By the time he was called, Newman's father was unfit to give coherent testimony. Interestingly, the evidence he did manage to deliver, unequivocally supported the Rector's case.

Though Foster walked from the court a free man, his character was tainted and was forever labelled a philanderer. But if his character was dealt a mortal blow it was nothing to that of Sarah Newman's mother who, according to the Rector's defence, was supposed to have provided an outlet for the village's sexual tensions at her house opposite the Congregational chapel!

What then of this charge made against Simon Quy Viall and Gardiner and was there any foundation to it? At the time of the accusations Viall farmed land at Lower Hall Farm that stretched from Foxearth to the neighbouring village of Pentlow. Edward Gardiner, also a farmer was Viall's drinking partner and may have been a willing accomplice to any of his friend's ideas that came out of past dealings with the Rector. There had been a history of tension between the two men. From the time he arrived at Foxearth, Foster

---

[9] The Sessions where Foster was a magistrate and sometime Chairman of the Bench

began to buy up most the land in the village including a substantial piece of land once farmed by Simon's grandfather Alfred Pratt Vial and which would later be farmed by his son Samuel. Only according to land deeds Alfred did not own the land. Indeed it had been falsely sold to him by auctioneers Richard Pettit and Samuel Hills at a Bargain & Sale Fair in September 1840. Soon after the sale, the land was snatched back by Executor's acting for the late Thomas Fitch who realised that the land was part of their late client's estate. When the disputed land came up for sale again, it was bought by one Mary Inch whose daughter subsequently sold it to Foster.

The younger Viall's perhaps had good cause to think that the farm land would be leased to them but instead the Rector leased it to a William Chinery. This may have been nothing more than a simple business transaction but it may have upset the Viall family enough to give them reason to spite Foster. Though this connection is a mild one, it is nothing to that of the extraordinary tale of what happened after Samuel Viall died in 1855. The following is a blow-by-blow account of the peculiar story of the burial as told by the Haverhill Echo:

It appears that the late Samuel Vial, who was a wealthy Landowner and Farmer, residing in the adjoining parish of Cavendish, died on 23rd. of Sept. 1855, then leaving two sons and a daughter (married), and it is alleged on one side, but contradicted on the other, that on his death bed he desired to be buried in Foxearth Churchyard, but whether so or not, he was buried there, and soon after a dispute arose between the deceased's friends and the Rector (Rev John Foster) with reference to a tombstone or memorial to be erected, as they wished to erect over his remains.

The incumbent states that the proposed monument was a column surmounted by a wheat sheaf, the whole to be surrounded by a railing, and he therefore objected, considering it unsuitable; he was then threatened with proceedings in the ecclesiastical court, and a correspondence ensued, but ultimately a simple tombstone was erected.

When the late Mrs Vial died, her sons wished her to be buried alongside their father, to this Mr. Foster consented, although she was not a parishioner at the time of her death, on condition that a written agreement was given that they would not erect any tombstone until the design had first been submitted and met with his approval. The Rector states that his object was to prevent any disputes arising afterwards. As the sons refused to give the written guarantee, Mr Foster objected to the burial taking place, and Mrs. Vial was interred in Belchamp Otten churchyard.

The matter rested for a few months, until Mr. Simon Quy Vial and Mr.Pratt Vial, the two sons, applied at the Chancellors Court of the Diocese of Rochester, for a faculty to remove the body of the late Mr. Vial from Foxearth to Otten Belchamp.

On Wednesday morning a number of men from adjoining parishes assembled at Foxearth, and remained there until two o'clock, when Mr Jasper Cardinall of Halstead, solicitor for Messrs Vial, arrived with the faculty. A hearse was also there, with some stonemasons from Messrs Keogh's yard at Sudbury, and labourers to help disinter the coffin. The gate of the churchyard was locked and the men remained outside on the meadow. Mr Cardinall read the legal document and demanded the body.

The Rector refused on the ground that the faculty being invalid; and said that otherwise he had no interest in the matter, other than to protect the interests of his parishioners, especially Mrs. Ewer, a parishioner, a daughter of the late Mr. Vial, who as well as her children wished the body to remain at Foxearth. Mr Simon Vial denied that his father had expressed a desire before his death to be buried there.

Mr Cardinall made a speech in which he alluded to the un-Christian and uncharitable nature of Mr Foster's refusal to permit the disinterment of the body to where it might lie alongside his wife. At one time there was quite an uproar, and it was feared that the men would proceed to take violent steps to remove the body, but Mr Cardinal allayed the storm, and a portion of the crowd, which had increased to some two hundred people who vented their feelings in giving three groans for the Rector, and three cheers for Mr Cardinall and Messrs Vial.

We understand that Mr Foster expressed himself perfectly willing to permit the removal of the coffin if legal faculty was obtained. The grounds of the objections to the one produced, was we believe that no citation had been produced or issued to let the objectors come forward.

The memorial on which it had been obtained also stated that the applicants had obtained the consent of the Rev. Dawson, Rector of Belchamp Otten, for re-interment in his churchyard. This is denied, on the other side it is alleged to have been given verbally. However written notices were served on Tuesday, on Mr Vial, not to proceed to inter the remains in Belchamp Otten Churchyard.

The Bishop of Rochester had also written to Mr Foster to say the faculty obtained was quite out of order, no citation having been issued.

It appears Mrs. Ewer had also protested and prayed the Bishop not to permit the removal. An order likewise was given by the Rector and churchwardens of Belchamp Otten not to assist in any manner.

No attempt was made to disinter the body, and about five o'clock the hearse and the men left the ground, and the crowd dispersed. We hear it is intended to take proceedings, and that the matter is likely to cause considerable litigation in the Ecclesiastical Courts.

Samuel's body was later exhumed early one morning and re-buried in Belchamp Otten churchyard though the perpetrators had charges of body stealing and sacrilege lay against them. However, it seems the crime was not fully investigated and the charges were later dropped by the order of the Rector. Simon Quy Viall eventually sold Lower Hall Farm for £3000 in 1862 to real estate agents Oakes, Bevan & Co in which the Rector's brother George Anthony Foster was a partner. On its sale Viall returned to his other home at Baythorne Hall at Birdbrook, Essex, where he died in 1885.

The central character to this plot, John Henry Foster, was born into a patrician family at Liverpool in 1815, the eldest son of John Foster, whose father William had been an important architect in Liverpool and was nick-named the 'King of Liverpool' owing to the number of buildings he had designed for the city which included

Lime Street station.[10] His mother Margaret Troutbeck,[11] was the daughter of William Troutbeck, a very wealthy merchant and an influential man, partly due to his supposed lineage to King John.

John Henry inherited a large fortune from his grandfathers and father and throughout his lifetime courted the rich and powerful. He spent his early years in his home city, was educated privately, went in due course to St Mary Hall, Oxford, and entered the church.

His first curacy was at Kempston, Bedfordshire in 1844 where he married his first wife Rosalind. She gave him three children, two of whom would die before the age of three. He was instituted to the living of SS Peter & Paul, Foxearth, a year later in 1845 - the same year a good friend and fellow Tractarian John Henry (later Cardinal) Newman converted to Rome.

Up to the time of his death, Foster was domestic chaplain to the Molyneux family, who were Earl's of Sefton and lived at Croxteth Hall[12] near Liverpool and one of the grandest estates of its day with farmland stretching for several square miles.

He earned praise for his pastoral diligence and with his huge legacies he turned to architecture on a cardinal scale. As Rector he prettified Foxearth's mediaeval church, demolishing the south aisle; provided the £900 to build the school and commissioned various items of church plate and stained glass window. He was devoted to the welfare of his parishioners, making no distinction between those who attended church and those who attended chapel and was at the forefront of turning over some of his land behind the school to enable villagers to grow their own crops; this at a time when farmers were often reluctant for their men to grow vegetables, on the grounds that work that should be going into their own crops would

---

[10] On his death in 1846, William Foster left an estate worth in excess of £300,000. Rev John Foster received £30,000.

[11] She died in 1862 leaving an estate of at least £200,000. The money from the estate was used to buy property in various villages (including Foxearth) and paid for alterations to SS Peter & Paul, Foxearth.

[12] Begun 1575. The Earl of Sefton was responsible for leasing land at Aintree for the purpose of horseracing and visited his Chaplain at Foxearth on more than one occasion. The Earl's nephew was priest at St Peter, Sudbury, 1847 – 1876.

be diverted into the labourer's own - all well before the Tysoe allotments and 'the Promised Land' were finally achieved in 1893 which tried to turn labourers into small-scale farmers in imitation of the continental peasantry.

Here was a man who stood resolutely for progress; he invested wisely even when his investments could be looked on as highly questionable for a churchman, and if the Bishop of Rochester had found that one of his vicars was investing in a brewery and a beerhouse, as he undoubtedly was, then there would have been serious, not to sat highly hilarious, consequences. He sidestepped this curious dilemma by signing over alcoholic interests to his brother, George who, so Trust documents make out, invested heavily in the fledgling brewery.

The socially adept George had made a large fortune out of a variety of financial interests including: banking, the law[13] and property deals and was an influential member of the glamorous Kildare Street and Carlton clubs in London. He had four children but seems to have attached quite as much importance to his own pleasures as he did to his family's and could spend 100 pounds on a new gun while begrudging his daughter Amy her evening dress. He took over his mother's house at Chilton Lodge near Sudbury on her death in 1862 and which she had bought in 1853 for the enormous sum of £2325.[14]

Although extant correspondence suggests men of desiccated emotions, the two brothers were genuine philanthropists as well as

---

[13] As a barrister, George practised both in East Anglia and London

[14] Chilton Lodge belonged to the estate of the late Major General Addison and was set in 3 acres. The General had died shortly after attending the funeral of the Duke of Wellington at St Paul's Cathedral. Addison was a friend of Wellington and had fought in many campaigns including Toulouse (1814) and Waterloo (1815).

Chilton Lodge was bought on Margaret Troutbeck's behalf by Jeffrey Blunden, Churchwarden at Holy Trinity, Long Melford. At the same auction he bid for and bought a further four acres adjoining the Lodge for £380 and a 'fine period house' for £500 where George Anthony Foster lived until his mother's death in 1862. Chilton Hall was presented to the Rev Andrewes, (John Foster's father in law after his marriage to his daughter Elizabeth) in 1863.

being shrewd businessmen who would have leapt at a way of finding work for local people and knew a good investment when they came across it. Altruism though was not always the case with some members of the family. George's wife Georgiana was in favour of litigating the smallest offence. On March 5, 1872 she obtained a summons against a boy named Jarvis for damaging her dress by kicking mud on it as she was leaving church. The boy turned out to be the son of a gentleman's coachman and although Georgiana withdrew the summons she said the boy deserved to be whipped. Her idiosyncratic qualities led George in private to give her the nickname 'Bird Brain' which he usually contracted to 'BB'. Georgiana to her credit seemed, in correspondence anyway, not to mind.

His brother's much loved first wife Rosalind had died within five years of their marriage although he seems not to have been victim to Victorian coyness. Indeed, he seems to have been positively irresistible to women and passion quickly overtook his mourning when he began to court 16-year-old Elizabeth Andrewes who enjoyed some local celebrity on account of being a member of the Andrewes', a well-known family who lived at The Aubries in Bulmer - one of the richest estates in north Essex.[15] Through careful patronage they, the Fosters and the Molyneux family, were contemporaries, as were most of the tightly knit East Anglian squireachy. But they did have a lot to live up to - the better known member of the Andrewes family was the Squire of Bulmer, Robert Andrewes, who along with his wife was painted by a 22-year-old Thomas Gainsborough.

John Foster was a good friend to Elizabeth's father (The Rector of Bulmer) and although the family were rich, much of their wealth was tied up in property. From surviving records we know that the rector lent the family money; later waving the debt in exchange for Elizabeth's hand in marriage, perhaps as part of a complex dowry arrangement – they married at Foxearth on Elizabeth's 18th birthday.

The proof that associates the Foster family to the brewery and the Ward's is clear cut. The indisputable evidence comes in 1894 following the death of George Anthony's heir his grandson William

---

[15] Rev Andrewes had previously lived at Little Waldingfield

Francis Foster, who had died twelve months earlier. George had entrusted his estate to his brother John, his son Henry Marshall Foster and Henry Crabb Canham, a friend and solicitor who was a partner at Andrewes, Andrewes and Canham in nearby Long Melford. Sadly both George and his son died in the same year[16] leaving Canham as the only surviving executor to the estate, proceeds of which were to go to George's wife. That July he instructed the Sudbury auctioneers George Coote and Son to auction off George's substantial ownership of the village. This included:

'numerous lots, the important Foxearth Brewery. Erected in the most substantial modern manner, with Brewery House, managers residence, extensive premises, beerhouse, gardens and paddocks, in occupation of Mr David Ward, under a repairing and insuring lease, having 15 years to run, from Lady Day next, when the entire property, with its accruing increment falls into the freeholder, thus rendering it an investment far superior to Consoles.'

And this was not the only property to go to auction. By agreement with her husband's executors[17], Elizabeth Foster had moved to The Cottage, now for auction came:

'several small occupations, 'Model Dwellings', numerous cottages and gardens, a blacksmiths shop, etc. forming almost the entire pretty village of Foxearth. .The advowson and right of Patronage and Perpetual Presentation to the Rectory or Parish Church of Foxearth, with charming residence and grounds, a highly restored and beautifully adorned church, about 23 acres of Glebe Lands, and commuted tithe rent charge of £ 443 per annum.'

Naturally David Ward was anxious that his numerous rivals would be defeated in acquiring the brewery and most of the other property. Within a short space of time he managed to secure enough funds to buy the majority of the Foster estate. He bought everything

---

[16] Rev Henry Marshall, curate at St Mary's Reading, died April 9 1885 aged 27; his father died 30 October the same year. Both are buried at Foxearth in the Foster family plot.

[17] William Henry Irvine (nephew) William Francis Foster (grandson) who died 1893 and Henry Crabb Canham (family solicitor).

except the rights to the living of the parish, the church, rectory and glebeland. The brewery and land was bought by private treaty for just £1600.00 the rest of the estate for little less than £10,000.

Intercessionaries including Elizabeth Foster helped the deal through, with the proviso that the necessary money would be paid in one lump sum. Unfortunately Victorian obscurity precludes us learning anything more but it is likely that with Marshall dying without issue and William Francis not being around to administer the family business, Canham thought it appropriate to sell the majority of George's assets and keep Georgiana in the style to which she had become accustomed. No doubt her sister-in-law, Elizabeth, thought it sensible to sell the land on which the brewery stood and majority of the glebeland abutting it including Black Apple Tree field[18] and Bareland Lane[19] together with the village blacksmith's forge in The Street.[20]

John Foster's final Will contains nothing alluding to the brewery but one dated December 1889 does. Earlier that year, on August 22, he hired land and the brewery on a 21-year lease to David Ward with the proviso that the brewery was insured 'against fire for at least £400'. Two years before his death in 1892, Foster made sure that money raised from the sale of his lands (on which the brewery stood) would go to Elizabeth providing she did not remarry.

Towards the mid-1890s, Ward & Son's beer was dramatically increasing in popularity and George Ward had been able to afford his children a small private education and perhaps left behind a fair inheritance for his wife and dependants but it is hard to see how these could have been enough to have brought the family a fortune.

---

[18] Black Apple Tree field was bought in 1862 from Frederick William Bethel who lived at Mole End Place. It was later re-named The Playground after John Foster designated it common land and bored a well on the site for drinking water. It is now pasture land.

[19] Bareland Lane is opposite the entrance to The Chase in Mill Lane, Foxearth.

[20] Set up by Henry Ives in the 1850s. The site was redeveloped and a grace and favour house built for the head brewer. Once called Sunnyside it is now called Magnolia House. A new forge was built for the brewery in Mill Lane to shoe dray horses and make various ironwork.

At an auction shortly after the private deal, David Ward bought a further five cottages in the village (opposite the village school) including the one which he had been renting from George Foster's trustee, for £4 a year.

Although not of the same social standing as some of his peers, Ward was very well connected and would not have found it a problem to find wealthy individuals keen to invest in the brewery - this could have included members of the East Anglian squireachy such as the Bull and the Andrewes' families as well as their friends. Certainly the money required to buy the brewery and adjacent estate would have been more than he could have raised on his own, so sufficient share certificates may have been issued, and enough of them to allow the village to stay in a preferred owner's hands.

When local newspapers broke the story that other investors had been involved in funding the brewery and it wasn't just wholly funded with the Ward's wealth, it accelerated an enormous fanfare of invention and suspicion.

It was widely rumoured that the Rector had had an early dalliance with Charlotte and that David was John Foster's son. Certainly the pair had a close father and son relationship but there is no absolutely no evidence to support anything other than this. The only ingredients were gossip and hearsay which when combined usually makes for a random deduction. In any case, it seems that George Anthony may well have contributed more to the Ward's enterprise than his brother did, and it appears that he supplied the necessary funds to build the brewery on his brother's land. Today, there would be no consideration given to this most basic form of asset management. The Rector was one of the very few clergyman of his day, and maybe since, to part own a brewery and by leasing his land and investing some of his fortune in it and encouraging his brother to do the same, started a classic rags to riches story for the Ward family. If the scheme had failed they would have left their hopeful heirs little besides the reflection that John Foster was not the first prelate to have found a monument in profligacy

Foxearth Brewery in 1886

THE COPPER YEARS

As the firm of Charlotte Ward & Son drew to a close, Ward & Son and its heir, David Ward, came of age together. Fittingly, the celebrations that marked, in effect, the commercial birth of the business and David's 21st birthday in 1880 were held inside the first purpose-built brewery. This spartan building at the rear of The Lion beerhouse was constructed by relatives of his mother, - Mortlock's of Cavendish. The builder of choice, they carried out all additional work on the brewery's expansion, well into the 1940s.

The size of a large barn, the wooden louvered brewery housed a four-comb brewing plant, comprising two fermentation tanks, storage space, a brewing copper which could hold up to 60 barrels of liquor and a crude refrigeration unit which enabled beer to be made throughout the year.

The copper was an expensive steam-heated closed device that had the immediate benefit of being faster to come to the boil, and used less base material to begin brewing. The task of brewing was most likely shared between David and his mother with the work of shifting barrels and other manual work done by Fred Cousins - a native of Stoke who settled in the village after marrying his Foxearth born wife Eliza Ward, one of David's nieces.

Their supplies were drawn from local farmers such as Alf Thompson at Borley; John Butcher of Bulmer and William Inch of Windmill Hill at Foxearth with Branwhite's supplying malt and hops. All three farmers, or their descendents, were occasionally supplying the brewery at least until 1907 and were tenants of John Foster and his heirs.

Of all the styles of beer available around this time, Ward's 'common type' or 'cheap' draught was the most popular, though others such as the popular porter were making them good money.

Even at this early stage most of their beers used sugar to maximise the alcohol content and keep nitrogen in the beer which contributed to its clarity. Sugar as a malt substitute was now becoming a commonplace ingredient in most brewer's list of raw materials though curiously its popularity by brewers had led to hefty taxes whilst at the same time, a tax on malt had been abolished.

Their cask ale was generously hopped and as it had been brewed with sugar it took on a high alcohol content. This quickly found favour with the beer drinking public. XXXX Strong Ale continued to be made well into the 1950s. It was certainly the outstandingly popular beer in the area with an average original gravity of 1056. From this moment on, the Wards must have realised that they had a triumphant success on their hands.

By 1886, after considerable refining and perfecting of their products, the brewery installed a bottling plant, which when it went into production that year was churning out 300 bottles of beer a day.

Now the firm was second only to the much bigger company of Whitbread to hand-bottle its own beers on a commercial basis. Success had a marked effect on the business as it began to capture the all-important nationwide market for its products. Twelve months after the line was installed the company was inundated with orders for their beers and the work to get orders out on time was unstinting.

The early installation of the Worsnam engineered bottling line was on a trial basis, and several modifications to it had to be made as the demand for Ward's beers doubled. Later that year the beer was chilled and filtered to avoid secondary fermentation in the bottle as it passed through a revolutionary Carlson and Seitz cold-filter process. This had the benefit of cleaning the beer and producing a brighter and cleaner tasting product - adding proof that Ward's products were unadulterated. This was an adventurous concept but theirs was an age of forward thinking. New ways of working and new ways of life abounded. The mobility of the rural population was also increasing with the building of new roads and the coming of the railways it simply made travel more desirable and the carrying of goods easier for all, which allowed many industries, including the brewery to tap into untried and widespread markets.

Improved transportation and communications, such as the emergence of a reliable letter system, opened communities out to wider influences and new experiences; the next decade was to see great development in the Ward's fortunes. In 1888 rapidly increased trading required the building of a large scale brewery, which stood just a few hundred yards from the original.

Part of this many-windowed red-brick edifice was given over to a yeast room and it is here, thanks to advanced microscopy techniques, Ward's began to experiment with notoriously temperamental top fermenting yeast strains. It was Pasteur who had established beyond doubt that yeast was a living plant and that only active cells can bring about alcoholic fermentation; it was this process that was so vital to the brewery and testimony to this can be seen in copies of Ward's early brewing books.

At each stage of the yeast growth, the head brewer would rigorously check and control a series of filtering, cooling and dilutions, reheating and acidity testing with the aim of producing yeast that had the perfect characteristics to brew beer with. Ironically Ward's continued to buy-in most of their yeasts possibly as their experiments were often haphazard and erratic. A note made by David Ward inside one of firm's brewing books says 'Pitching yeast: Very few cells formulated and several dead cells.' Then asks in exasperation: 'Do something Mr Brewer. Head Brewer tried to clean up lab. I ask, hopeless.' Why the brewer had to clean up the lab is anyone's guess. David Ward was a dictator, but a benevolent one with a sense of humour.

Shortly after the incident, he wrote a note to his workers that the never ending objective of the brewery was to achieve products of the highest degree of quality and purity and the 'skilful management of yeasts.'

It was always characteristic of him to thank his employees personally for services rendered by offering them his hospitality, and over the years the tradition of an annual excursion, usually to London, had grown up at the Foxearth brewery.

The Suffolk Free Press, often invited along to the outings gives us an idea as to what the events were like:

On Wednesday last Messrs Ward and Sons, brewers, gave their annual outing to their employees numbering forty. London was the place decided upon. Through the kindness of Mr Bedford, stationmaster at Long Melford, a special saloon carriage was arranged for the conveyance of staff. Mr Fuller who chaperoned the party, made arrangements for breakfast on arrival, which, it is needless to say, ample justice was done to after the early journey. The morning meal over, some visited St Paul's Cathedral, whilst others went and saw their friends but most of the party went on to Madame Tassaud's and were greatly delighted with the wax models, so realistic, especially to some who had not visited Baker Street before. At 12.30 all met and visited the Earls Court Exhibition and dined at Spiers' and Pond's fine dining saloon, where a capital spread was served presided over by Mr D Ward, who was supported by Mr W.H.A. Barnes, late brewer to the firm, and Mr H.B. Bailey of Cambridge. Mr Leggott taking the vice-chair. After dinner various places of amusement in the Exhibition were visited. At five o'clock all met again for tea, and the remainder of the time up to 8.30 was spent in the grounds. The homeward journey was made very pleasant with toast and song, Mr Ward not forgetting the refreshments. Mr Leggott proposed a very hearty vote of thanks to Mr Ward on behalf of all the employees, remarking that it had been the most enjoyable day they had ever had. Mr Ward suitably responded, saying it was the largest party he had ever taken out, which was very gratifying to know that the increase of employment meant increased trade. In his remarks he made some very kind allusions to all who had assisted him during the past year and thanked one and all for their services. A special word of praise was given to Mr Fuller for efficiently carrying out his duties as brewer, Mr Fuller responded in appropriate terms. The singing of Auld Lang Syne brought a very happy and memorable day to a close.

Soon his committed staff would devise a number of farsighted and innovative products to widen the market and create loyalty to their beers - but large capital was required to fund their next venture.

Although the previous seven years had seen their wealth mount, the family did not possess the required money to expand as fast as they wished, so the wealth of their backers was keenly felt in October 1891 when two artesian wells were bored on glebeland in the village.

This then was expansion on a big scale, with considerable cost. But it had to be done; the water the Ward's had been using was brackish and contained too much organic matter which could have resulted in bacterial infections, turning a pleasant pint into a stomach ache.

The huge bedrock of chalk throughout Foxearth was a Godsend as the material acts as an organic filter which purifies and softens water.

Engineers located the chalk level just fifty two feet from the chosen site and bored to a depth of 330 feet where the water table was sufficient to provide exceptionally pure water, similar to the water table at Burton on Trent and perfect for producing some of the best pale ales for which it would become famous. What a blessing it must have been that the water threw no lime deposit on boiling.

The wells, bored by Isler and Co from Southwark, London, were capable of supplying 2000 gallons of water an hour and a special deep well steam pump, made by Barton and Company of Sudbury was commissioned. The pump was one of the most modern of its day; The East Anglian Daily Times describes it as being "of the deep bucket and plunger principle, counter balanced with rising main working rods and enclosed in a bore pipe carried down to the source of supply some 80 feet.'

This system of procuring water is now considered the most perfect yet devised, the water being pumped pure and bright direct to the tanks at the top of the brewery from the deep water bearing strata immediately before use. We believe this is the only arrangement on this system in the neighbourhood.

Messrs Ward & Son must be congratulated on the success that has attended their indomitable pluck and enterprise, as the whole undertaking involved great risk, attended with heavy expense.

Now that the brewery had an independent and copious supply of sweet water, minds were turned to hiring a leading brewer. After a selection process lasting several weeks, the firm had decided to employ the services of brewer and chemist W.H.A Barnes from London who had previously worked for Collier Brothers at the Essex Brewery at St James Street, Walthamstow.

The task for Barnes was to develop beers on a mass scale, turning away from the heavier gravity beers that people were used to drinking. Real strides had been made in brewing science since the method given by George Ewart Evans and much more was understood about how yeast converted sugars to alcohol and carbon dioxide and how varieties of hops and different malts altered taste. Barnes also saw that the then fashion for mineral water would turn a heavy profit especially as drinking water was highly polluted - advertisements offering Foxearth water as of the 'highest standard of purity for pharmacoepia' soon followed.

This was a time when taste was being developed by the London publications that percolated through to the villages. The local newspapers, though still read were not instantly seized on as were the monthly periodicals, such as the *Illustrated London News* and the Graphic. Hugh Jessopp, a writer for the fashionista's favourite, the *Graphic*, summarised the changes he saw about him in the late 1880s.

> *The truth is that the peasantry have begun to develop new tastes as well as other people; they have shorter hours of work, i.e. more leisure, the women seem to have passed out of the labour market altogether. I have found them reading novels; they like to see things looking pretty, they put up neat papers on their walls and they have an art for fashion.*
>
> *Food is changing too. It has to be nutritional and not too clumsy. People demand that food is made from the best fresh and natural ingredients and all sort of drink is lighter and fresher tasting, especially pure unadulterated water. All this is so much gain.*

One of the chief problems of more leisure time was that villagers in some villages had nothing to do except drink and get drunk. Entertainment was slight and usually homespun. With some exceptions, squires, farmers and churchmen disapproved of any social gathering that were not under their aegis, where disaffection might thrive. While village inns and alehouses which the farmers and squireachy patronised were seen as respectable drinking places, the ordinary beershops were seen as sinks of depravity and sin.

After iniquity, drunkenness was the prime target of Victorian reformers; which presented something of a quandary for the good Rector. Here was a man that had closed down the village alehouse, built a church school in its stead and was not only now investing in making alcohol but also owned a beerhouse in which to sell it from.

In the last decades of the nineteenth century, temperance movements such as the Band of Hope were successful in persuading many children and adults to sign the pledge of teetotalism. Although he was not a fervent supporter and regularly peddled his favourite saying 'Let responsible men have freedom of thought to what is right in God's eyes', to still possible controversy, he knew that he must be seen to be upholding standards. However, since he was bankrolling the brewery he could hardly close it and certainly neither Charlotte nor David would have had the means with which to buy him out.

The following story from the Bury & Norwich Free Press shows how, as Chairman of the Bench at the Petty Sessions at Castle Hedingham, the court responsible for licensing and trying minor offences, Foster neatly side-steps a nasty predicament for his tenant.

In connection with the granting of licences - to Mrs Ward of Foxearth. The Chairman, the Rev J Foster said a caution was necessary. Supt Elsey said one night a man was found drinking beer supplied from her beer-house on the highway, but the police did not find enough evidence to bring the case before the bench. Rev Foster said he had enquired into the case and found that three men had not been drinking on the highway but discussing politics, being election time.

What a showman ! Though it is not surprising that after so many months of hard work that required villagers to keep it all in, at important festivals of the church year and election times it seems, villagers resolutely let it all hang out.

One moment that remained of supreme importance in the countryside was the end of the harvest. Around the mid-nineteenth century decorous church festivals were substituted for the rowdier secular 'Harvest Homes' or 'Horkeys' of old which Foster supported ardently. The occasion was something vital to the self-respect of the community and provided the focus of a whole week of merriment. If abandoned, as many of these old traditions were in other villages, bad luck was thought to reign.

The following story from a copy of the Haverhill Echo in 1883 shows how at these 'Horkeys', the Rector was able to indulge in one of his local investments.

The Rev Pressey, curate, proposed a toast to the Rev John Foster, who was slightly indisposed due to ale. The first toast

41

was to the Church and Queen, second toast to the health of the preacher. Colonel Palmer of Liston Hall, proposed a toast to "masters and men", he said masters must not just pay a just wage, but do what they could for the interest of the workers, and the men must reciprocate. Much useful and common sense was given by the gallant Colonel.

As they drunk, two toasts were sang out 'Here's to the success to the bright ploughshare, and may it never rust' and 'May the beers next year be as good as this year.'

The same newspaper carried one of the first advertisements for Ward and Son, who were calling themselves ale and stout brewers of Foxearth, Essex. This would be the start of a long-running publicity and marketing campaign, stressing the range of its products which included: strong ale (XXX) brown ale, brown and mild; brown dinner ale, pale ale; amber ale; light tonic bitter and 'highly nutritious' stout at around 9 per cent ABV. These draught beers were available in Kilderkins (18 gallons) Firkins (9 gallons) and Pins (4 ½ gallons) only.

An agency to promote and distribute the beers was soon opened at A. Clements, 41 Chapel Hill Stores, Halstead,[21] with a further distribution and outdoor beerhouse opening at Alphamstone near Bures the following year, with the newly opened store of Holland and Barrett stocking beers in Sudbury. Ward's also hired one James Hostler as the firm's first traveller.

Now as a director of the brewery, David Ward had his first experience of running a large-scale industrial enterprise that called on his talents as a publicist and marketing man. Curiously, he sidestepped any mention to the press about how his father had first started the business, nor did he speak of the importance played by his mother, Charlotte. This may have been nothing other poetic licence but face-to-face interviews with David in later years regaled readers with immaculately tailored reflections omitting any mention of his parents - a trend which became established detail.

For all his shortcomings, and he had so very few, David Ward sounds the note of a gifted and thoughtful man. He was educated at a

---

[21] The beerhouse at 41 Chapel Hill, Halstead, was sold in 1919

small private Dame school in Long Melford by a Mr Zechariah Payne and took a keen interest in rural affairs. Throughout his adult life he valued the sturdy principles of self-education and self-improvement; the latter was a strong force throughout the working classes in Victorian society and village reading rooms were one of the commonest projects of philanthropically minded businessmen, although they were often regarded with suspicion by some villagers.

In Foxearth's case however, local effort alone wrought a revolution in the intellectual life of the village.

On February 29 1889 the Essex & Suffolk Free Press reported the opening of the village's reading rooms:

On Tues. evening last a pleasant gathering took place at the School room (Kindly lent by the Rector) to inaugurate the opening at the "Village club and Reading Rooms", A capital meat tea was provided, to which a large company sat down, the Rev Foster kindly taking the chair. After ample justice had been done to the good things provided, the chairman in a few well chosen remarks, explained the object for which the club had been started; reading the rules, and promising his very valuable assistance. Officers were then duly elected as follows:

President: Rev Foster

Treasurer and Secretary: Rev Marshall

Committee: Messrs: Inch; Hostler; Piper and Maxim

Curator: D. Byford

Daily, Weekly, and illustrated papers are provided, also books, bagatelle, draughts, and other indoor games. It is also intended to promote outdoor amusements consisting of quoits, football and cricket. A hearty vote of thanks was given to the rector for kindly placing the rooms at the disposal of the members and also to the Rev. Marshall for the trouble he has taken to promote the interests of the club. Mr. J. Chickall, Mr.C. Ray, and Mr. D. Ward were also present and kindly added their names to the list as honorary members. About 30 names are already enrolled as members; which promises well for the future at the club. The party broke up at eleven o'clock after spending a most enjoyable evening.

The final chapter in the life of the architect of so many things was not a happy one. In the early spring of 1892 Foster's health deteriorated slowly rather than suddenly. He had been suffering from syphilis for some time and this was now complicated by bronchitis. His death was unhurried and lingering. During the night of March 17 he experienced difficulty in breathing and his body became feebler. By the morning of March 18, it was all over.

He had been Rector of the parish for forty-seven years and was the force that shaped it. When he arrived at Foxearth in 1845 he quickly realised the derisory nature of the existing village and set about re-organising the parish to the betterment of its inhabitants and he was, notwithstanding the gossip, and his sometimes triangular love life, devoted to their welfare. [22]

On the morning of March 22 1892, his 'massive, mediaeval coffin of polished oak, panelled with massive brass furniture' was laid to rest next to that of his long dead daughter, his first wife Rosalind, his nephew Henry Marshall and his brother George. Foxearth church was filled to overflowing with many mourners having to stand in the churchyard. That nagging sense of anti-climax and unfinished business that often surrounds the burial of the dead did not arise. The congregation, which included 'a large number of ladies' heard that their parish priest had turned his apparent deficiencies into virtues which, allied to a strong character, enabled him to dominate the imaginations of so many friends, admirers, acquaintances and detractors.

The Victorian rural clergy typically aligned themselves with the interests and point of view of the squire and farmer. As a class they so closely identified themselves with the gentry as to give the impression that they regarded themselves as a sort of spiritual squireachy, which left them outside the real modern life of the village. Foster had come to Foxearth at a time when to many villagers it must have seemed that their whole world was owned and

---

[22] Fidelity was not one of Foster's virtues. A first hand account has a young lady arriving at her aunt's cottage unannounced. Going into her aunt's bedroom she disturbed her aunt and Foster in a state of some confusion. Keeping a cool head whilst fastening up his trousers, Foster made the inspired excuse that her aunt had fainted and he was trying to revive her.

ruled by those they worked for and their masters expected absolute humility from their social inferiors which no doubt led to many clashes of will and personality.

His devoted work changed this attitude and made a real difference to the parish. Most of his parishoners, it has to be remembered, were people who lived a life of unending toil and frequent domestic chaos, their lives advanced only slowly, but by his investing in various local projects there is clear confirmation of better living standards in terms of a more varied diet and possessions of small luxuries such as watches and bicycles.

Five years on in 1897, the year of Queen Victoria's Diamond Jubilee, Foster's former brewing empire displayed more excited growth. On September 1st Charlotte Ward cut the ribbon at an elaborate topping out ceremony in the newly built brew house block and handed the reigns of the business to her son David, making him the company's first chairman. Although she had been an innkeeper at The Lion (having received its on-licence in 1890) she had spent fifty out of her seventy-three years guiding the brewery from its modest beginnings.

What a great distance the business had travelled in the four decades since Charlotte and George had begun brewing in 1848. The rich man at his castle; the poor man at his gate was the ordained social order of the Victorian village and to question it was to question God's will; but within that structure there was room for movement.

It was easier perhaps, to slip down than to rise up. Essentially, though, the social structure of the village was static, certainly compared to our fluid society. Everyone from the landed gentry to the labourer knew their place. Farmers showed elaborate deference to squires, labourers tugged their forelocks to their employers. However, David Ward represented a new rising gentry based on industry rather then land[23]

At the brewery, the brewer held status above all but the directors and formed a class above the rest of the workforce, though those

---

[23] David Ward had moved from his rather cramped accommodation opposite the school, to Carbonel's Farm

there with a special skill, such as the cooper, lifted themselves into an exalted position.

This visible prestige came from a successful business and move up the social ladder meant huge benefits for the immediate area and beyond. During this period, the industrial history of the brewery, sees workers arriving not only from nearby villages such as Glemsford, Cavendish and Clare but faraway towns such as Stoke and Newcastle.

For an agricultural village such as Foxearth which had witnessed the tragic fiasco of the Swing riots[24], the dwindling dominance of the land owner and his old-fashioned arrogance was to be celebrated.

Now fresh employment prospects introduced new and higher standards of pay and afforded people dignity. By the close of the century and the end of Victoria's reign, the old patterns of village life were breaking under the strain, and would soon be swept away.

The opening years of the twentieth century (there was much debate as to whether it began on 1 January 1900 or 1901) brought the widespread use by the better-off of electricity, telegrams, automobiles and many other luxury items. The village saw the infancy of mass communication in 1901 when the brewery's first telegram arrived from Long Melford announcing the death of Queen Victoria.

Two years into the new century on February 28 1902, Charlotte Ward died after a short illness. She was seventy eight. Her death, fittingly at the Brewery House (where the offices stand today), was keenly felt - surely more so than the prosaic voice of the South West Suffolk Echo makes out:

The funeral of Mrs Ward (widow of the late George Ward and mother of Mr David Ward) whose death occurred on Tuesday at the Brewery House, took place on Friday afternoon. The deceased lady was one of the oldest parishioners, and until five years ago was associated with the firm of Ward and Son.

---

[24] The Swing Riots erupted throughout East Anglia after being fuelled by desperation at low living standards, low wages and underemployment caused by a stagnant demand for labour but a rapidly increasing population.

The Service throughout was conducted by the Rector, Reverend W.J. Pressey.

Before its commencement Mr C Sillitoe who took the place of Mr David Ward on the organ played O Rest In The Lord. The hymns sung were A Few More Years Shall Roll and Abide With Me. The psalm was sung to Felton's tune. The lesson was read by Mr J.C. Lambert. The choir sang the Nunc Dimitis and Mr C Sillitoe played the Dead March from Saul as the cortege left the church.

The mourners were Mrs Oakley, Mrs Youngman from Walsham Le Willows; Mr David Ward, Miss Ward [sic], Miss Winifred Ward; Master Bernard Ward, Master Harold Ward and Martin Bailey, Cambridge; Mr T Leggart, Mr Farrance the Haverhill agent and the brewery staff and employees. A number of parishioners also attended. Mr Rice of Cavendish was amongst those present. The panelled oak coffin bore the following inscription and breast plate:

In Loving Memory of Charlotte Ward
Who died Feb 25th 1902
Aged 78 years

Charlotte was buried in Foxearth churchyard next to the grave of her late husband George and her nephew George Ward Miller (a former brewery worker) who had died from typhoid in 1899 aged twenty four and whom Charlotte had adopted.

His mother's death must have had a powerful and profound effect on David especially as his own wife Louisa was seriously ill with cancer and would die from the disease two years later, aged 48.

He had good cause to look back over his parent's past achievements with a certain degree of pride and satisfaction. People from a modest background had somehow turned from being small-time brewers into running one of the most modern breweries in East Anglia, if not the country.

Now David was in charge of shaping a flourishing, successful business that was proving itself against fierce opposition. Indeed, in the early 1900s almost every village had its own brewery supplying the local pub trade - Long Melford; Ballingdon; Chelmsford and Halstead plus dozens more a few miles away.

He would have to outdistance them not just in quantity of production but in quality of taste. What set David apart was how deeply Victorian values had left their mark on him. He was motivated by the age's progressive philosophy and was committed to the pursuit of excellence; his position in the village did not blunt his appetite for hard work.

A paternalistic but progressive employer, Ward provided the best working conditions he could finance and his concern for the welfare of his workers ran deep. However, one of his eccentricities was his insistance that his workforce had to be Anglicans who went assiduously to church on Sundays. Dissenters, such as the religiously emotional Baptists and Methodists, whose yearnings of the soul were unfettered by rigid forms were avoided. Methodism especially, had sprung from the very class it served and made Christianity a living force within the community rather than a power over it with hymns stressing eternal salvation rather than temporal justice, their rousing words and tunes encouraged a spirit of self-confidence, self-reliance and self-respect and perhaps this may have marked some worshippers out as potential trouble-makers. Every form of dissent, notably of religion, was banished as one strain of churchmanship soared above all others, even then it was not always possible to protect the brewery's largely Church of England workforce from unseen dangers, as this story from a copy of the 1903 Haverhill Echo makes out:

There was an accident at Foxearth brewery, a man named William Gowers of Glemsford was engaged in what is known as turning the beer, whilst doing so his apron got caught in a revolving shaft which runs through the room where he was working, he was drawn in to the moving machinery and spun round two or three times, fortunately his shirt and other clothes gave way and released the poor man who then fell several feet and was caught by a workmate before he hit the ground, he was seriously injured and was carried home in a horse and wagon [sic], he is so badly swollen that Dr Waring cannot know the injuries. The facts are that the man's father in law is also lying dangerously ill at his son in law's house.

Alas, nothing is known of William Gowers fate. Barring the occasional accident, the brewery was the favoured place for local people to work. It paid generous wages supplemented by a beer allowance and ran a bonus system, giving employees a small share in the brewery's profits, and sometimes other allowances in kind, such as fuel.

In a few years, almost all the cottages in the village would be bought to house the brewery's employees, and soon others would be built; rents were offered to tenants at much lower rates than in nearby villages and a real effort was made to make the village a healthy place in which to live and work.

It has to be remembered that it was a rare place that was free from disease. Most villages in the local area were still unsanitary and the lack of a convenient or reliable water supply was a crucial health risk. Many cottages relied on dipping places or stagnant water which usually contained water-borne diseases such as cholera and diptheria.[25] In the wet months most of the cottages grounds would have been full of stagnant water and the whole village would have badly stank; open sewers running through the place frequently trickling down from the cottages into the small brook at the far end of Rectory garden next to The Street leading to Cavendish.

Damp houses brought on pleurisy and rheumatism, smallpox, scarlet fever, measles and whooping cough were common, consumption was rife.

G.F. Millin describes a serious outbreak of virulent diptheria at nearby Great Yeldham occasioned by the 'scandously filthy' condition of the village, 'suggestive of the London slums'.

In contrast to official apathy from the Board of Guardians who often acted slowly, grudgingly and ineffectually, the crisis brought out the best in the village notables, as this from the Suffolk Free Press on July 26 1903 makes out:

---

[25] A tragic outbreak of diptheria claimed the lives of five children (four from the same family) at Western Hall Farm, Western End. Their memorial stands in Foxearth churchyard.

In September 1903, Mr Ward made the parish of Foxearth a handsome gift by making public the supply of pure clean water from his brewery. Mr Ward has now carried his generosity further, for some time now the dipping places in the village have been deficient in supply and quality and last month that supply stopped altogether. The rector suggested to Mr Ward that perhaps he could send his waste clean water from the brewery across the road down through the village. To this Mr Ward agreed to do at some considerable expense to himself, within a fortnight the pipes were laid and water is again flowing through the village. There is a reminder that the water is not fit for drinking inasmuch as it is liable to surface contamination. We would ask all whom it concerns, to show appreciation of this gift, by doing all in their power to keep the dipping places clean, and the channel through which the water passes, free from rubbish.[26]

This sort of devoted work made a real difference to a village but his benevolence, although no means necessary, proved that an alternative to the usual creed of culture existed and this acted as an attractive incentive for men to stay in the village. All around them workers were becoming more migratory; the old stability of surrounding villages and the life in nearby market towns such as Sudbury and Long Melford, was beginning to be undermined.

The extraordinary loyalty and devotion David Ward inspired among his staff explains how he was able to achieve so much within a relatively short space of time. He comes over as a considerate, sensitive and humane man who though known as a martinet trusted and respected his employees, treating them generously, if not as equals, certainly as fellow human beings - an attitude unknown to agricultural workers.

---

[26] The arrangement to supply the village lasted until a meeting of the Belchamp Rural District Council on June 1st 1933 when David Ward told them that he had supplied the village for over 40 years and felt the time had come to have a public water supply. The village lacked a main sewer up until the 1950s and before flush toilets, sanitation meant human waste was buried in the garden or used on allotments as a cheap and plentiful manure.

Now men found consolation in the polished irony of being sought after. Hours of work were trimmed largely to suit better standards of employment. Consequently there was a mass migration of people to the towns and cities, primarily due to the insecurity of rural employment, low wages and workers being subject to summary dismissal. Without a doubt the loosening of the community ties, and the new sense of impermanence - change which informed village life - were not to be regretted.

Broader mental horizons enabled villagers to move beyond - or simply move away from - the 'stagnation of narrowness of mind' which Richard Jeffries saw as souring village life. He wrote:

Backbiting is the curse of village life, and seems to keep people by its effects on the mind far more effectually in the grip of poverty than the lowness of ways. They become so saturated in littleness that they cannot attempt anything, and have no enterprise.

A modern brewery in a rural setting may sound out of place but the industrialised village was no new thing. As it was, Foxearth was typical of many villages in which agriculture was beginning to be more of a peripheral activity; it marked the beginning of the end for squire-led industries and rigidly hierarchical posts. For the first time in living memory there was regard for workers whereas in the past they may have been hired for the summer and turned into the workhouse for the winter, with as little thought as someone today putting their lawnmower away for a season; now workers were needed to power the new economy and new industries such as the railway, engineering (Whitlock's at Great Yeldham), flax mills (at Liston) brick works (at Bulmer), textile factories (Sudbury), feed mills (Long Melford) and a host of different industries, unfamiliar just a decade before.

David Ward's radical ideal reflected the new social dream - employees receiving a regular wage with clean housing and running water; a self-contained world in which nobody was idle; few people in absolute want, in which there was no squalor nor hunger - Arcadia realised.

His own life was not without tragedy and after Louisa lost her battle with cancer, David sought refuge in one of her closest friends,

Mabel Constance Andrewes,[27] a loving former companion and nurse to his late wife and niece to Elizabeth Foster. By the spring of 1905 David had proposed and when the couple married in style at Church of St Mary Abbots, Kensington on October 3 later that year, it brought the alliance of two distinguished families together. Maymee's adoptive family grew to adore her, the older children welcoming her more as a stepsister than surrogate mother.

Two years later and motivated by increasing demand for Foxearth beer (there were agencies all over the Eastern Counties including Ipswich, Felixstowe, Dovercourt and one in Finsbury Park, north London) the June of 1907 witnessed further construction at the brewery and a sad end to The Lion. The building had witnessed many central emotions and events. It was the birthplace of David Ward; there his father had gambled his livelihood and made a successful business; it had been the substantial comfort for Charlotte Ward and supported her fragile life after George had died; but in this forward-looking age there was no room for sentimentality and it was demolished to make way for offices, a house and an off-licence. [28] At the west side of the brewery (in what is now The Chase) better-equipped cask-cleaning sheds and a long shed for storage were added which enabled the wooden casks to be steam cleaned rather than scrubbed by hand; the engine house was extended and a new boiler room housed a coal-fired boiler that had been fitted in 1904. Measuring 32ft 6in by 8ft 6in and weighing 26 tonnes it was nicknamed 'Big Win' By the middle of the year the brewery was a rambling conglomeration and took up nearly two acres of land.

The extensions to the building proved absolutely necessary. In 1908 at the Brewers Exhibition in London, Ward and Son won their

---

[27] Maymee's father Canon J.B Andrewes and wife lived first at Little Waldingfield and then Prospect Place in Bulmer. The latter was bought with a £100 mortgage arranged through David Ward and paid off at 4 per cent a year.

[28] The off-licence was managed by Ursula Coleby who lived at South View in the grounds of the Ward's house The Cottage now Hunters Lodge. She was a member of a well-known village family. Her husband Lewis was gardener to David Ward and their son Ken was later to become a good friend and bat-man to David's son Harold. South View was demolished in the 1950s.

first gold medal for their Imperial Pale Ale which in a few years would become their flag-ship beer.

The Suffolk Free Press commented that:

Messrs Ward and Son, brewers of Foxearth are to be congratulated on achieving the distinction of being awarded first prize and a silver medal with a diploma for their pale ale at the Brewers Exhibition in London last week, the highest distinction in the bottled beer competition, which is open to all in the United Kingdom.

Some 300 samples of beer were exhibited in a variety of classes from breweries all over the country including some from celebrated and well known firms. Messrs Ward's well known productions already command a large sale throughout the Eastern Counties and beyond, and the distinction now conferred, reflects great credit on this progressive and enterprising firm.

At that year's annual company outing, David Ward (known as Kruger or Old Dad) told his workers the brewery was barely holding its own against tough opposition and a bad harvest. It was a critical time for the industry. Records show that nationally there were five hundred fewer breweries in 1908 than there had been at the turn of the century. The 1904 Licensing Act of Balfour's Conservative administration did not help matters.

This draconian and predatory law targeted uneconomic pubs and saw the magistracy close down others simply because they believed too many served the same area. This confused Act badly affected breweries that relied heavily on captive trade. Disillusion was ameliorated for the owners who received some reimbursement from the Compensation Authority. In less than twenty years over 20,000 licensed houses were abandoned and although many of the closures were premises that were truly unprofitable, suspicion settled in amongst some in the brewing fraternity that a few justices were running a small-minded campaign against public houses and favouring licensed clubs.

David Ward experienced the Act at close quarters on more than one occasion but one pub of particular note was the Eagle at Whelnetham. According to the *Suffolk Free Press*, the magistrates at the Brewster Sessions held at the Shire Hall, Bury St Edmund's, heard evidence from the police divisional Superintendent that the pub was experiencing a waning trade and should be closed down.

Supt Brunning had said that the present licensee (Mr Lewis Elmore King, an ex-soldier) had been in occupation for three years. The rent of the house was £73, and the rates came to £23 6s 8d. It was a stone and tiled building, with a cottage attached, and comprised bar, living room, a cellar, a hall and three bedrooms with an outbuilding formerly used as a brew house and now utilised as a shed. The property had a fair share of trade and the average trade of the house was 2¾ barrels and 4½ dozen bottles a week. In summer the average mineral water trade was eight dozen bottles. He did not complain of the trade and said he made a fair living.

Witness thought King a good tenant. From the Rushbrooke Arms to the Victoria was 395 paces; from the Victoria to the Eagle about 785 paces; from the Eagle to Bradfield Manger was 1½ miles by the main road. There were half a dozen cottages within 200 yards of the Eagle, nine being a quarter of a mile away (Cox's Green) and four or five in Water Lane, also a quarter of a mile distant.

Cross-examined by Mr Ashton (Ward's solicitor): Is it not a nice countryside house ? Is it very convenient in the summer for cyclists ?

Supt: Yes, but few people live there.

Is the house in the midst of three important farms

Supt: Yes

Did you enquire of the tenant what sort of customers he had ?

Supt: No

Is it the only house Messrs Ward and Son have in the neighbourhood ?

Supt: Yes

Now perhaps you know something better (laughter) - do you know Messrs Ward & Son's beer is very good

Supt: Yes

Do you know they have taken several prizes

Supt: They might have done

You agree with me that doing three barrels a week trade is good trade ?

Supt: I was surprised at the amount, yes.

You agree that the Eagle is very convenient at Harvest Time and within easy reach ?

Supt: Yes, it is

Mr Ashton, addressing the bench said that if the full facts had been known at the Licensing Sessions, the present case should not have been brought before them.

The Chairman of the Bench, William Hervey, briefly reviewed the evidence given and said that it would be a pleasure to renew the licence. The main point was that the Eagle was doing a good trade, and was required to meet the demands of the neighbourhood.

Despite this reduction in the market, the company survived the hard times, beating the critics who had predicted the brewery would be a casualty of the downturn.

That year, Ward's paid a total of £4442. 6s beer duty on 12, 370 barrels brewed (a barrel equals 36 imperial gallons) and £4577 10 s and 9d duty on the next year's 12, 795 barrels brewed. Is it any wonder times were hard.

Three years later in April 1911, at the International Exhibition of Hygiene in Paris, the company pulled off a remarkable coup in British brewing history by becoming only the second UK brewery to win the Grand Prix and Gold Medal with Diploma for their Imperial Pale Ale and Oatmeal Stout.

Part of the victory was due to a chemist named Harold Heron who had devised a composition that was added to the brewing liquor. Although various chemicals were being added to the water or wort around or before the turn of the century, Heron updated a chemical water treatment that would improve on those already in use for heavy beers such as stout and pale ale. His blueprint, which included sulphate of lime; chloride of lime; chloride of magnesium and salt, laid the way for brewing riches.

The brewery in 1912

THE GOLDEN AGE

From 1909 the brewery had exploited the London trend for soft drinks and these too were winning admirers and prizes. Flavours such as stone ginger-beer, dry ginger-ale and lime juice captured the public's imagination and trade was buoyant. Soda water was a favourite Edwardian mixer and Ward's supplied it in grand style by making the siphon head in silver-plate - the insides lined with porcelain. In the autumn of the same year Ward and Son won a major contract to supply the National Sanatorium with 'nutritious oat malt stout' and mineral waters, which gained great popularity owing to the Sanatorium eccentrically approving the beer as part of the daily diet for convalescents. It was from this success that much of the power of Ward's marketing was to stem.

Other large contracts supplying national institutions, including various regiments of the British army such as those based at Landguard Fort at Felixstowe and the House of Commons flooded in.

Dancing around with these triumphs, the company knew that more space was required if it was to expand satisfactorily. David Ward toyed with franchising the brand to Bailey and Tebbut at Panton's brewery at Cambridge, [29] but was encouraged by his good friend Harold Bailey to have an immediate rethink. In 1912 he gambled on designing an updated version of the three-storey brew house originally constructed in 1897, and commissioned by his mother.

This new Mecca to brewing would house nine copper-lined fermenting vessels, the largest of which would hold 150 barrels in addition to a new laboratory and malt store and updated hot liquor tanks.

---

[29] Both Harold Bailey and his brother Martin served their brewing pupillage at Foxearth and remained great friends of the Ward family. The Panton brewery was the first to win the Paris Gold Medal for outstanding beer. It was awarded in 1907.

The brewery replaced its older coppers with one of 800 gallon capacity; the contents of which were pumped to the top floor of the brewery through condensing units and then to fermenting vessels below.

Originally the power source in the 1888 building was steam-generated, now a compressed air 90 HP diesel National engine was introduced in addition to two Lancashire coal-fired boilers which required the building of a 75 foot chimney stack. The transport fleet was upgraded and included four steam wagons and twelve horses with eight drays and carts, housed in stables and cart sheds beside two paddocks for the horses with an additional 10-acre field gifted by Eliza Foster which provided foodstuff for the hard-working animals.

A larger fermenting and conditioning room (nicknamed The Titanic Room) was completed in 1912, as were larger draught beer cellars which were capable of storing 2,000 barrels of beer. A new Long Shed was built to store 54 gallon capacity Hogsheads and here workers added finings - the process of producing a bright beer by adding ingredients such as isinglass or gelatine. A new bottling store had seven men and five women producing 1000 bottles of beer a day from two filling machines and the firm began bottling Gaymers Norfolk Cider. [30]

The firm now acquired new purpose. With the brewery at full production, most workers were working double shifts to cope with the exceptional demand. And what a demand there was. In 1913 the company sold 1900 barrels and close to 41, 000 bottles of beer. That year had several notable happenings. The brewery, according to the Suffolk Free Press 'eclipsed all records' by being awarded the championship gold medal, the most valuable in show, for their Imperial Pale Ale in Cask. They were also awarded a silver medal for their oat malt stout. It was the largest brewing exhibition the country had seen with over 440 exhibitors.

The beer was now suitably advertised as the 'National Beverage' and the firm began to diversify into selling wines and spirits. Ward's

---

[30] The brewery had a telephone installed in 1912 - the first call was made by David Ward to Lower Hall on August 28th at 11.00 am.

also brewed their first and only branded beer called Quilter.[31]Though it sold a respectable 279 barrels, and was made without added sugar, its popularity flagged and was subsequently dropped from Ward's range, sadly never to make a re-appearance.

The brewery's future in the hands of the family looked unequivocal with an heir waiting eagerly in the wings. George Bernard Ward was born in 1891 and by 1914 was already working for his father after finishing his education first at Malvern and then graduating to Queen's College at the University of Birmingham where he was studying brewing science.

Photographs show Bernard as a tall, athletic young man with impressive looks - very much the scion of an English middle class family with a practical and pragmatic side to his nature.

In the firm's old brewing journals, in some of which he caricatured his father, Bernard comes over as a sober reminder to the gifted that it is not so much the possession of a talent which is remarkable, as the ability to channel it. He was a social arbiter and like so many of his distracted age, his future seemed golden. He was active in village life, hosting entertainments and sports, where he excelled at cricket.

The donation of a recreation ground in the village by Reverend Kendrick Foster (nephew to John and Elizabeth) meant that a guarded form of battle against local villages was maintained following the formation of cricket and football teams. Bernard was a frequent captain of Foxearth Singles versus Foxearth Married. The singles usually won by many runs, no doubt boosted by their greater virility.

A particularly affectionate tribute was paid to him at his coming of age party. This, the Suffolk Free Press of 1913 tells us included 'a sumptuous repast which took place in the newly erected bottling plant and was followed by the presentation of a gold watch'

---

[31] From the Latin word 'cuilte' meaning 'mattress or cushion'. David Ward had earlier trained as an upholsterer. The name is possibly a genuflection to his former trade.

The Brewery Staff c1910

THE DARK AGE

The village's first mass industry, outside farming, had offered not just Foxearth but the whole of Essex a remarkable experiment in pluck and enterprise. Tuesday, 4 August 1914 brought that joined world of content to an abrupt halt and the stability of village life was to receive its quietus on the bloody fields of the Great War.

Four days later on August 8, the first of a series of regulations which were to cripple some breweries, called the Defence of the Realm Acts (DORA), were introduced.

Part of the Act gave local courts the capacity to regulate the opening of licensed premises in areas that were considered 'sensitive' such as those near army barracks. By October licensed premises all over the country had to close by 10pm at the latest. The problem for brewers was worsened when duty on beer rose from 7s 9d to £1 3s a barrel; the following April this was raised to £1 5s. And the swingeing measure did not stop there; by April 1918 the unstoppable upward momentum had reached £2 10s a standard barrel. A shortage of raw material also had the brewery producing a beer called Special, a malt-less brew, strong enough one would think to banish any gloom.

The majority of raw materials were in such short supply that anything and everything that would make a good ferment was called into use for the making of mashes.[32]

As well as having to cope with his many periodical business worries, David fought against a prolonged domestic distraction when his eldest son Bernard announced he was volunteering to fight. In the early summer of 1914 David said goodbye to the 22-year-old zeitgeist before he was to board a train at Sudbury railway station on his way to London for an onward passage to Guernsey and finally France. For his part, Bernard placed a lily of the valley in David's coat to remember him by. It was a sad day at Foxearth.

---

[32] The basis sometimes included boiled potatoes, potato peelings; anything and everything that would give a good ferment and convert into sugar and then alcohol was called into use.

Like so many young men of his age, Bernard must have felt a united purpose in a war against tyranny and was buoyed by the euphoric jingoism. The broad consensus and balance of belief about the rightness of the war was not fundamentally eroded over the next four terrible years.

When hostilities were declared, he first enlisted in the Army Service Corps as an acting sergeant in the Field Ambulance Corps before being commissioned into the 9th North Staffordshire Regiment (Service) (Pioneer) which had been formed at Lichfield on 20 September 1914; after a period of leave, he was taught to fly at the London and Provincial Private Flying School of Aviation and secured his ticket of efficiency in a swift nine days which tested his responsiveness to adjustment. Bernard made a couple of trips back to the local area in his aircraft before he was ready for active service. A report dated from the Essex Free Press on December 1st 1915 tells how a week earlier he landed his 45hp, French-made Caudron aeroplane at Lyston Park.

The visit of Mr. Bernard Ward of Foxearth who flew from Farnborough on Friday afternoon, created considerable interest in Essex as well as in Foxearth, Sudbury, Melford, Lyston and adjacent villages. Mr. Ward setting an example to many, who are claiming to be "indispensable", joined the army in the early stages of the war and is now an efficient "Manbird".

Aeroplanes have been from time to time passing in the vicinity of the town, but none have flown over the town as this one did. The throb of the engine was distinct as that of a motorcycle a street or so away. He flew low to salute the inhabitants of Sudbury no doubt, and they were out in crowds, for they knew who it was. After giving Sudbury a greeting, the machine sped off to Lyston, where numerous friends were awaiting. He alighted gracefully in the park at Lyston.

On Saturday he made several flights over Melford and Sudbury, encircling several times. A large crowd was in the park, morning and afternoon to see the ascent and descent, and to inspect the machine at close quarters. Mr. Ward took to the air again on Sunday and manoeuvred the machine over

Melford and adjoining parishes, and left for Hendon in the afternoon with the best wishes from his numerous friends.

Soon he was dispersed into a divisional unit and was seconded for duty with the Royal Flying Corps. He began serving in France from February 1916.

On Tuesday 21st November 1916, The Times newspaper stated that Captain and Flight Commander G.B.Ward, was awarded the Military Cross for conspicuous gallantry in action.

He flew over the enemy lines at a height of 100 feet under heavy fire, and carried out a very successful artillery reconnaissance, he has previously done very fine work.

After surviving several daring missions taking recognisance photographs, Bernard took off from his aerodrome at Cloque, on the Pas de Calais on September 21 1917 at 10.45 am together with his observer 2nd Lieutenant W A Campbell. Their objective was to photograph the German front-line. Shortly before 1 pm, ground observers saw his machine crash while fighting four German aircraft. He was mortally wounded and died at the scene and Campbell later died from his injuries. It was a world away from the beauty, peace and tranquillity of the English countryside. The final, sombre statistics of the war, 750,000 British servicemen killed in the carnage, another 2,500,000 wounded (many permanently) reinforced the belief that mass militarism should be rejected.

The war memorials which rose on village greens throughout the land after the cataclysm of the Great War, with their poignant lists of the old village names - five from this family, four from that, three from another - were a memorial too, to a way of life that was gone forever.

It was more of a memorial than the village was used to. For the vast majority had lived and died for the most part unknown, un-regarded and now their vanished world would keep its silence for eternity.

In a telegram to David Ward that arrived at Lower Hall on September 23, 1917, Lieutenant Colonel Carthew, Bernard's Commanding Officer, wrote explaining how his eldest son and heir, had been killed.

'Your son was killed in a fight with four hostile scouts today. His machine fell in our lines, and we recovered his body, but he died without regaining consciousness. His observer, Campbell, tried to land the machine, but it was completely smashed, and the observer sustained a compound fracture of the skull and I am afraid he is not likely to recover. Nothing that I can say to you will adequately convey the true sense of the deep affection and respect which all of us who worked with him and were privileged to know him well, entertained for your son.

He has been in my Wing since he first took command of No 10 Squadron, and has proved himself one of the best and most efficient, as well as one of the most popular, Squadron Commanders I have ever known in our Corps. As you know he loved his work. He has given you every right to be proud of him, and his loss to us is irreparable. For myself, I mourn him not only as a Squadron Commander but as a close personal friend of whom I was very fond, and I ask you to accept this tribute to him as an expression of heartfelt sympathy which is, believe me, deep and heartfelt. I have compiled a poem as a tribute:

I shall remember, friend of mine, the day
We walked for hours, and still I hear you say
Lapina I love - and the warm breeze of Spring
Bluebells and pools and sand and everything
That's clean and fresh. Paddling in pools - the sun
And taking Billy for a run
Could I but hear your laugh and see your smile
Or touch your hand and talk to you awhile
And reconstruct those plans as oft before
Those wondrous schemes for life 'after the war'
You steeled yourself - and laughed at shot and shell
(You played the game magnificently well)
I shall remember to my dying day
You gave your life - to help and show the way
Tonight is fine - a full moon and the sky is filled with stars
You're almost sure to fly,
the hum of your machine will soon pass by
Do you remember all those wondrous nights ?
The fun we had with navigation lights.

And when returning from the East and West
Far overhead you'd flash a merry jest !
But all is still - there's not a sound and I
Remember that somewhere in France you lie
Asleep. In Goggenheim - it is close by...
Oh! France - Great Mother - You, who watch their sleep
We thank you - and our gratitude is deep
For the great vigil you so reverently keep.

Bernard had been awarded a bar to his Military Cross a week before he died. In David Ward's own press cuttings book is a letter written by Maymee to Bernard on the day before he was killed. Full of the everyday hum of life, it arrived back at Foxearth three days later marked 'Killed In Action'.

His father, dispirited, at first abandoned the brewery in lethargy and despair and likened the news of Bernard's death to the cutting of a ring of bark from a healthy tree. Escapist longings, never far distant, threatened to overwhelm him. The crushing psychological and moral impact of such an appalling loss as his adored son must have profoundly coloured his isolation and outlook. For all his acuity of loss David dragged his weary body back into commerce. Bernard was not the only young man from the village and surrounding area who had died. Throughout the war David had sought to keep members of his workforce at home and attended many tribunals to argue their cases in front of a military judiciary. Altogether Foxearth lost 11 men and one woman whilst fighting in France. Three of the men died when they drowned in the mud of Flanders, after torrential rain.

Now the plans for developing the business had to be re-thought and David's younger son Harold came into the equation. He too was serving as an airman in France and had been shot in the leg in 1917. On getting airborne again a few weeks later, he and a comrade were shot up in a dog-fight by the infamous Rittmeister Manfred von Richthofen -the Bloody Red Baron which resulted in Harold being severely wounded and invalided back to Foxearth.

The long, bitter war of attrition that the generals predicted would be no more than a short, swift textbook manoeuvre was to end a year later. When peace returned, it seemed that little had changed. But it soon became disturbingly clear that life was not normal and the comforting framework of pre-1914 could not be easily restored. In the spring of 1918 Harold followed in the footsteps of his brother and went to study brewing science at the University of Birmingham and later achieved first-class honours in the subject.

Although the brewery, like almost every other industry, faced disruptive economic problems that resulted from the loss of markets, a loss of manpower and further increases in duty (after the war duty rose to £3, 10s a barrel), David Ward seems to have been an employer who was careful in his financial activities and one who inspired loyalty, trust and affection. The war had brought misery to the Ward's domestic life and the business was waning with reduced consumption of beer in many areas of their empire.

There had been authoritarian governmental controls over the opening hours for licensed houses; prices had been fixed and brewers were asked to reduce the original gravity and consequently strength of their products - the average original gravity for Ward's in the war years was 1030 o.g. Worse of all breweries had been requested to brew less beer as well as being compelled to use poorer quality base ingredients - Excise duty too had climbed ever higher to raise further money for the costly war effort.

It was a dark age. David Ward could have reacted by embalming the business in a nostalgic light but instead set about issuing a series of challenges to himself and his workforce. New patterns of production were formed that would shape the future of the brewery for the next two decades.

Part of this new approach involved becoming a public limited company following tight profit margins and one year where David had been forced to put much of his own money into the business in order to balance the books. In June 1919 the ambitious moment arrived with David and his son Harold becoming directors of the new firm called Wards Limited, they floated the company and issued forty thousand shares at one pound a share; money which they used to expand their portfolio of cottages, land and expand the brewery buildings. That same year the company brewed 13, 617 barrels - an incredible achievement given the extremely difficult circumstances in which they were operating in and an increase of six hundred barrels immediately before the outbreak of war.

No action more effectively expressed the mood of renewed optimism than strengthening their captive trade which they did by buying up further licensed premises. The brewery's estate of the early 1920s included: 21 licensed houses and 15 various clubs and off-licences under the Ward's stewardship. Part of their retail estate incorporated the business of retail brewer George Frederick Grice at the Cock and Bell public house, Long Melford. At that year's annual Brewer's Exhibition, Wards Limited walked away with the show's highest honours by winning a gold medal for their new Burton Ale as well as collecting a silver medal for their Imperial Double Brown.

The nature of Foxearth remained; a new world nodding with familiarities of the old. The census of 1921 shows that the population was not tempted away from the village by higher wages abroad or in far-flung towns and cities and the brewery was very much the king-pin in that.

When Elizabeth Foster died the following spring, the long, close and active interest the Foster's had given to the parish, the Ward family and the brewery, was all but over. The identification of the church with its middle-class values, with the family, the community and a safe form of patriotism was alive that day - funerals were one of the few areas of village life where members of different classes socialised together and school children, shopkeepers, brewery employees, the landed gentry and practically everyone from the village lined Lime Walk in serried rows and streamed through into the church.

David Ward, now as a member of the family, helped to bear Elizabeth's coffin as it was laid beside that of her dead husband. Sarah Newman, the girl who had accused John Foster of raping her and whom Elizabeth had found a position in London, stood by her graveside and wept. [33]

Back in the wider world even the terrible cycle of industrial decline in the mid-1920s with rising unemployment and social bitterness that led to the worst explosion of class conflict Britain had yet known, failed to harm the brewery's renewed profits even though the price of a pint had risen to an astronomical 7d.

---

[33] There was an insatiable demand for country girls as servants; they were considered more pliable and trustworthy than town girls.

This can partly be put down to David Ward's inner radar knowing that the future success of his business relied on a co-dependent and happy workforce. The extension of his charity to local people was a crucial ingredient to the brewery's continued prosperity. Acts of kindness were not always in the form of grand gestures; he allowed village women to use boiling water from the brewery on their washdays in the days when clothes were scrubbed in wooden troughs. Most cottages had no sinks, and of course, no running water or electricity.

The brewery supplied the elderly with whisky, beer and food at Christmas. David Ward personally bought the village cricket team a pavilion and was generally responsible for funding the construction of the Foxearth's Men's Club in Love Lane, now a comfortable house. Some years later in January 1928, he donated land to fulfil his ambition of building a village hall and gave all of the money required except for £170. The hall was dedicated to the memory of his dead son, Bernard.

The *Suffolk Free Press* takes up the story:

Foxearth Village Hall was formally opened by Mrs St Leger Glyn, on Wednesday evening. Mr David Ward, chairman of the building committee, said it was his cherished dream to see the hall opened, it was only two years ago that they formed the first building committee, now they were in their brand new hall.

Mrs St Leger Glyn, said that it was with real pleasure that she came here tonight, she declared the hall opened and Mr Ward presented her with a box of chocolates and a bouquet of carnations. The Rev Basset, treasurer, said that they had collected £ 754 12s 9d, by means of fetes, whist drives and subscriptions, the cost of the hall was £ 787 10s and they had paid the builder that amount less £ 100, which they owed him, they had spent £ 250 on furniture and roughly wanted £ 125 to be free.

Mr Basset said he thought the reason that village halls had sprung up everywhere since the war, was that the men in France had got together more than ever before. Mr Basset thanked Mr Ward for all he had done, nobody knew how much time and money Mr Ward had put into the hall, he had doubled what had been collected, in conclusion, the speaker thanked the anonymous donor of the electric light installation.

The hall was designed by Messrs Hunt and Coates, Architects, of Bury St Edmunds and was built by Messrs Grimwood of Sudbury. It measures 50ft by 24ft, the outside is rough cast, panelled with massive oak posts. There is an entrance which forms a cloak room and leads through double doors into the main hall. Behind is a spacious kitchen, fitted with cupboards, sink, tables, stove and all necessary apparatus for provision of teas which will be served at whist drives etc. The water supply is laid on from the brewery and sanitary arrangements for both ladies and gentlemen, are of the most modern type and are connected with the main sewer of the village.

The hall is furnished with folding hard wooden chairs and folding card tables, it is lighted by the Kohler Automatic Installation as sold by Messrs Dixon's, Motor Engineering Company of Sudbury, the first switch sets the engine in motion and the hall is immediately flooded with a brilliant white light, the installation is of the most up to date form of lighting and obviates the need for storage batteries. The indoor decoration is cream with a four foot dado.

The hall is well lighted and is ten feet high at the eaves, the ceiling is covered in and the acoustic properties are effective.

The business committee was:

Mr D.Ward (chairman) Mr C.Hurst (secretary) Rev G.H.Basset (treasurer) Messrs H.E.Ward A.Maxim F.Levick E.Harper F.Woods, S.Eady. Contributing to the following concert were F.Cornish H.Ince H.E.Ward (vocal solos), W.Coote (comic songs) Mr Broyd (saxophone and violin) The Foxearth Trio (H.E.Ward-A.Maxim-F.Rush) sang old English songs and Pearce's dance orchestra.

The Twenties ended in a haze of nostalgia and innovation but warnings lay ahead. David Ward must have been a reassuring figure in those times and comfortably locked within the village embrace. An acceptable touchstone for a community struggling to preserve a traditional order in the swirling tides of post-war transformation.

It was a confusing time. The national mood at the turn of the decade was grim and the crash in the American stock exchange in October 1929, followed by a downward spiral of trade and employment, was beyond any government to correct with unemployment reaching almost three million. This was partly due to the history of low investment, over-manning and inefficient work practices, intensified by a culture that for decades had elevated gentlemanly conduct above business education or enterprise.

Confounding the national mood there was to be no industrial stagnation at Foxearth. The consensus of Ward's beer drinking public was enthusiastic and a further 210 foot well was bored at the Pinkuah Arms in Pentlow which the Ward's had bought that year from the Bull family[34]. Whether it was a speculative buy and they expected to build a brew house on the licensed premises or pump the water to Foxearth is not known but in any case the pub was sold twelve months later.

By 1931 the 50th anniversary of the first dedicated brewhouse the glowing affirmation of success saw the brewery producing 400 barrels a week and 12,000 bottles of beer a day with ever increasing loads on the mineral water business. Work had begun on new engine rooms (complete with a Rushton Hornsby engine); a powerful ice plant (which later contained the most advanced condensers) and a newly equipped fermentation department. It capped a 57 year period of generally uninterrupted growth and profits.

A feature article on the brewery in the Sudbury Free Press sketched the firm's modernity at the peak of its 1930s untiring output.

A business to be a success today must be abreast of the times, and Foxearth brewery is out to meet the demand for lighter, more brilliant and sparkling beers, compared to the heavy gravity beers of our forefathers.

The brewery is capable of producing four hundred barrels a week, while the large and well appointed bottling stores have facilities for supplying no less than a thousand dozen bottles a day. The spacious cellars have an enormous capacity for

---

[34] From the Estate of Felix Bull

thousands of barrels of beer. Those intended for bottling are kept in store for six weeks to two months to mature. Everywhere the plant and machinery are up to date.

Almost every village family had at least one member who worked for the brewery. Foxearth was a steadily growing community and in a variety of ways at peace with itself and enlivened by an industry run by people with great imagination.

The 1936 Brewers Exhibition brought yet more success for the Foxearth firm. Out of 743 entries including entrants from all over Britain, India, Canada, South Africa and several large and important breweries in the U.S.A. Ward's further endorsed its quality of beers by securing a championship Gold Medal for their Imperial Pale Ale.

It had been a triumphant exhibition and was a timely success, for the domestic mood was to change within a year; not through any immediate local or national disunity but again through the external impact of foreign affairs.

Two years later on 1st September 1939, Hitler took the fateful step of invading Poland. After a few desperate attempts to patch up a last-minute compromise, two days later Chamberlain announced Britain had declared war on Germany.

As twenty years earlier, the village and country regained its sense of unity and national purpose amidst the challenge and turmoil of total conflict.

A new war was to have serious repercussions on the brewery's business. The previous year David Ward had laid out significant capital when the brewery bought a new centrifugal Worsnam pump to replace the previous model that had been used in one of the original wells since 1897.

In the same year war was declared, a 400 feet deep well had been bored a few months earlier, which had been a necessary but costly affair, lined as it was with 200 feet of 9 inch quarter inch thick galvanized steel tubes by Brown's of Ipswich; the water pumped by a Lea Howell pump. This had upped water capacity to a further 3,000 gallons of water an hour. Now the brewery was able to call on 120,000 gallons of water each working day.

No one knew quite how long the war would continue for, so as markets began to contract violently there was the inevitable shortage of brewing material; this in turn led to Ward's immediately withdrawing supplies of the best-selling Imperial ale which in turn meant the House of Commons was forced to remove its 25 year patronage.

As though to emphasise the imminence of great change, David Ward, renewed his punishing early working regime at the brewery where he was still chairman. Although in his early eighties, he visited the brewery each day and spent at least two hours touring the brew house and talking to his workers. Once on finding analytical tests on the brewery's water supply, which were carried out annually by Heron's Laboratories in London, he vented his dismay towards the head brewer Trethowan.

On Heron's analysis certificate he wrote, in stark red ink: *"Why wasn't I told about problems with the new well - 'I knew nothing of these [tests]. Why not?'*

Not everybody found this proud and difficult presence winning. A note in one of the brewery's books announced unkindly: *"Boss came in. Usual bloody-minded self. Bombastic and boring."*

War-time measures made for heavily less economically successful production than before, with the result that one local brewery G..E Cook at Halstead, made an abortive attempt to buy the brewery in September 1943. Although the austerities of war-time Britain had a deep effect on the brewery's output (it was down to producing 8,500 barrels a year in 1944) the average original gravity of its beer was a weak 1021, the firm managed to keep good trade and employed the same amount of workers as it had at the outbreak of hostilities including its invincible head who had an aversion to retirement and looked on work as 'one of the finest tonics on this earth.' and was still typing all his own letters at the age of 88.

Yet three years after victory, not even the ministrations of work could rouse him. He was a little over ninety years old, and died according to his death certificate, of congestive cardiac failure, coronary arteriosclerosis and hypertension - that is heart failure, aggravated by the narrowing of the blood vessels possibly causing angina and high blood pressure without any apparent cause. The liver was blameless, and he died, as he had lived, by the heart. It was the same year that his grandson, David Harvey Ward was receiving his brewing tuition at Gilstrap, Earl & Company of Newark, Nottinghamshire. His grandfather had spent sixty-nine years developing a business that by today's standards of growth would have been vying for a Queen's Award for Excellence, now his grandson was ready to play a new part in the firm that his namesake had taken an active interest in all his working life, and when most men would have long retired, continued as managing director up until his death.

When he was finally laid to rest in the presence of his many family, friends, villagers, employees, household staff and others it was next to his daughter Winifred who had died in December 1946. in a grave near to the church organ he had played for forty years,

The Suffolk Free Press wrote a loving tribute:

Mr Ward was slowly laid to rest not far from the organ he played for over 40 years. Mr Ward founded the well-known East Anglian firm [sic], he was 90 years old.

Canon Hughes referred to him as our friend and said that the life of our friend was long, also of the many activities in business, public work or the village in which he truly threw himself into with unbounding energy. David Ward tried to walk life's way with steadfast feet for the church of which he had deep affection.

He showed many extraordinary qualities. With his flair, intelligence and expertise, his reforming acumen, David Ward was responsible for providing the village with running water, electricity, leisure facilities and relative mass employment and probably equipped many other projects that are destined never to come to the surface. His business prowess gave Foxearth a more prosperous and egalitarian future. As an industrialist and entrepreneur he applied technology in a truly imaginative and sophisticated way, creating a brewery that would win multiple awards including 3 gold, 27 silver and six bronze medals - almost certainly the highest achievement for any brewery of any size anywhere in the UK.

Of course he served the public good, and with his ear for social nuance and distinction he helped to reform, whether he was sitting on the board of the Sudbury Board of Guardians or St Leonard's Hospital or as an elected member on both the Essex County Council where he remained for 21 years or the Halstead Rural District Council, where he was a councillor for 48 years.

In his will he left £38, 122 and asked his son Harold to 'guard, protect and comfort my greatly beloved wife, and always endeavour to bring sunshine and happiness into her life.'

The mantle of ownership was now passed to Harold, whose formative life had been somewhat frosted by his father's benevolent but autocratic regime. Intelligent, hard-working and accomplished, though he had been in nominal control of the company for over a decade his father still ruled the firm.

Outside work he was able and eloquent entertainer, beyond his articulate charm, a somewhat reluctant second chairman and managing director - although the latter title was not conferred on him until 1953. By all accounts, he had a tremendous talent for cultivating the public and like his father, was keenly interested in the welfare of the village - serving for many years on the Halstead Rural District Council, where he adopted his family's Tory allegiance and was chairman of the village hall committee, the parish council and a manager at Foxearth school.

A month after David Ward's death, rumour of a sell-out or a merger circulated the village. This time it was Tollemache's (later Tolly Cobbold) brewery at Ipswich that would be the wedding partner, with production moved across the border to Suffolk.

Although the rumours were denied at the time, contemporary accounts point to the rumour being uncannily accurate. The brewery had offered to buy out David Ward on numerous occasions and his death must have seemed the ideal time to broach the subject with his son.

G. Bernard Ward MC and bar

DECLINE AND FALL

The ending of brewing at Foxearth so soon after the principal's death would have been a terrible blow to the memory of a man that had striven to create an unbeatable, unblemished range of products and equally it would not have chimed in with the noticeable mood of optimism of post-war Foxearth. It may have been a reasonable economy at the time of hardship as rationing would continue for a further four years, but in the end the Tollemache takeover was repulsed and the Ipswich-based firm went back to their Suffolk headquarters and began the takeover process of smaller Essex and Suffolk breweries.

A few months after his grandfather's death, David Harvey Ward, became a director of the company following his successful pupillage in Nottinghamshire. After qualifying he shared the duties of head brewer with Ned Middleton, a highly experienced professional who had trained at Walter Gray and Sons brewery in Chelmsford.

At the 1952 Brewers' and Allied Traders' Exhibition at Olympia, the first since the war, the brewery found itself against an enormous record entry of brewers from across the country. In the stout class they were in competition with 50 others from the South Coast to Scotland, including some eight East Anglian rivals. David won the firm its first major award in open competition since the death of his grandfather when Wards Ltd was awarded first prize for their bottled stout.

For all that, the brewery in 1952 was poles apart to the one just a decade before. It was still winning medals but sales of beer were fast declining. They needed to borrow capital to sustain investment into promising new products but though still prosperous the business had not expanded along the same lines as others in the county such as the Romford Brewery. A straight comparison is rather unfair but in 1949, the year of its 150th anniversary, the Romford had 700 employees, 370 vehicles and 543 horses serving 44 provincial depots and 32 overseas. Foxearth was easy prey to a takeover bid. The firm's directors had already taken the steps to cut back on beer production and the selling of wines and spirits.

Then there was another hazard to consider. Many people in the trade were decrying the onslaught of lager, which although gaining popularity, only accounted for around about 1% of the market, but even so it threatened beer consumption. Now brewers had to place more emphasis on heavily branding their products. It was clear, even then, that the lager market was not like the traditional beer trade - it was all about being culturally sophisticated.

Like so many of its competitors, Ward's had concentrated their efforts on being a regional brewer and had not stretched their advertising much beyond East Anglia. They knew this had to change and mounted an aggressive marketing campaign and looked into developing a lager beer based on lambic yeast where the yeast is not manually added but is allowed to drift in from the surrounding countryside. [35]

This experiment was soon abandoned with the firm changing tact and turning to the mineral water operation, which at the time was on the verge of becoming a major brand. Within a short time new flavours were added to the range in order to cope with increasing demand – these now included: Lemonade; Cherryade; Grapefruit Crush, Orange Crush and Limeade. In 1953, the firm leased premises in St Matthews Street, Ipswich to act as a soft drinks distribution depot, but after a slow period of trading they moved the operation to the centre of town, eventually buying 95a Victoria Street.

One year on, the firm took out a franchise with the mineral water company Apollinaris, then owned by Gordon's Gin. The idea was to market novelty soft drinks that had tie-ins with children's comics such as Dan Dare. But before the company had the chance to develop this lucrative strand the deal collapsed after six months, victim of a German buy-out.

---

[35] This style of beer originates from Belgium. Due to the spontaneous fermentation, Lambic is a seasonal beer brewed only in the winter season (October-May). In summertime, there are too many undesirable bacteria in the wild yeasts, which can infect the wort and influence the fermentation.

So Ward's went back to production of its own branded soft drinks with turnover, the 1956 accounts tell us, a healthy £3,220 (net profit) or £50,000 in today's money.

These accounts[36] make interesting reading. The number of barrels of beer brewed was a diminutive 4,650, down on the 5,307 brewed in 1955. A huge drop from previous years, in fact it equated to production levels in 1890. The balance of the overall profit and loss account was a very healthy £45, 458 (roughly £700,000 in today's money) though this had decreased by £7,428 on the £52, 886 made the previous year.

Foxearth's balance sheet (fixed and current assets) show the firm's accountants had valued the brewery at £145, 391 (approximately £22 million in today's markets). Considering its size and prominence, the brewery was an extremely attractive proposition for those who had the money to be able to afford to buy it.

Not only would the buyer have a valuable asset but the company would have a prize name among its associated businesses and be able to do what it wished with the products in an ever decreasing market.

Britain in the mid-1950s saw a dispiriting mini-economic crisis thanks principally due to sterling emergency which led to the reduced purchasing power of the pound, consequently people were spending less - beer was a luxury not a necessity.

The hidden cost of the sterling crisis had taxes climbing disproportionately. The cost of brewing including beer duty rose to an all-time high, which greatly affected the brewery's economics; obviously this had some bearing on how the directors felt about continuing brewing at Foxearth. It wasn't that the business was under immediate pressure to sell, but the cost of brewing was escalating and sales were diminishing. In 1956 beer duty accounted for a shocking £38,785 of £47, 888 brewing costs.

This was a time when the large breweries were intensifying competition into the 'free trade' public houses. After a number of offers, including one by Cockburns which would have seen David Ward uprooting his family to live in Portugal, the directors of the

---

[36] Prepared by Ensor, Son and Goult of Ipswich

company decided to sell the company to Taylor Walker of the Barleymow Brewery, Limehouse in London; one of the liveliest companies at the time.

The London-based firm, under the guidance of Lieutenant Colonel Kingsmill,[37] had been buying up smaller breweries since the 1920s but had put on extra pace in the Fifties. In 1956 they bought out three rivals and Ward's was one of several in 1957. Others that year included The Victoria Wine Company Ltd and the Dunmow Brewery - a firm famous in its day for being one of the few without a beer allowance but permitting staff to drink as much as they wished whilst at work. David Ward would come to know it well, a few years later.

Taylor Walker officially took over the brewery and 31 tied houses and off-licences on All Saints Day 1957 with David now assistant managing director of the Foxearth branch.

When a presentation was made to Harold on his retirement as managing director, he made a speech to his staff telling them that they would keep their jobs now that the brewery had changed hands.

Although such proclamations were not over-optimistic, Taylor Walker's underlying strategy was to end all brewing at Foxearth within two years and to then use the brewery building to bottle Worthington, Bass and Guinness products[38]. Harold Ward made it abundantly clear that so much relied on the continued popularity for beer but whatever happened the buildings would also serve as a radial supply depot. This brought two distinct advantages to those who were employed at the brewery - they would keep their jobs and receive a pension when they retired. The latter reform swept away the fear of poverty. Just thirty years earlier the workhouse loomed for those unable to support themselves in later years; though it did provide for the physical needs of shelter and food it took away the self-respect of men and women whose whole lives had been one continuous act of unconscious self reliance.

---

[37] The Foxearth deal was struck by Richard Motion, father of Poet Laureate Andrew Motion.

[38] Ward's had at first been chosen to become the Guinness UK centre of operation. The deal fell through as it was thought the site was not near enough to London.

The brewery shortly before its partial demolition

ECLIPSE

The last brew of 62 barrels of Small Best Bitter Ale was made by David Ward on 19 February 1958 at a gravity of 1031. The attrition of the beautiful and palpable past was halted.

A farewell dinner for 56 employees took place in the July with several long-serving staff, some with 50 years service, picking up retirement presents from the board of directors.

Even so, not everybody was happy with the takeover. The Suffolk Free Press lamented the Taylor Walker deal and headlined their news story 'Obituary of a fine old beer' , it wrote:

Very shortly the last top will be removed from the last bottle of beer bearing a name that has been famous with drinkers for well over 100 years. The final consignment brewed has been delivered to the trade.

One of the last of the small family breweries, Wards of Fox-earth was started four generations ago by the great-grandfather of Director Mr D.H. Ward whose father, Mr Harold Ward, was chairman and managing director when the company was sold recently to Messrs Taylor Walker and Co Ltd.

The late Mr David Ward took over the business when he was 21 years old, and it expanded so rapidly that a new brewery had to be built next door to the original.

Twenty years ahead of his time in ideas and brewery plant and machinery, young David ensured that the firm was one of the first to bottle chilled and filtered beers, and that it always had the latest and best equipment available.

Result - prizes collected in the best beer exhibitions, year after year. The family brewery was formed into a limited company in 1919 and 30 public houses were purchased to form the nucleus of a guaranteed trade over an area from Wisbech in the north to Chelmsford and Maldon in the south.

But the name of Wards will not be lost completely, for they will continue to manufacture mineral waters for which they have already gained a reputation as being among the best produced.

Since its beginning, some seventy six years previously, the brewery had ridden dire economic times; it had collected a string of awards and more championship gold medals than any other brewery in the UK or continental Europe; it had shown that it was able to compete against the best in the world and had survived the interests of larger, wealthier firms and it had bonded the village into something approaching a true community with closely shared achievements.

But the perplexed brewing industry of the 1950s was one that was vulnerable to the immense strength of amalgamation and change. Now the brewery's vast halls would echo more to the sound of lorry engines and draymen's voices than that of staff on brewing days.

In an unexpected volte face, Taylor Walker themselves were absorbed by Burton-on-Trent company Ind Coope within 18 months - much it has to be said to David's regret and frustration. Feeling increasing disillusionment with the new set up and fearful that the Ward name would be destined for obscurity, he made up his mind to set up a reverse takeover and try to recover the firm's independence.

Although formal negotiations to buy back the main business began in July 1959 he did not meet Ind Coope management until October that year. Spelling out his intentions to Group Captain Carfoot, the Estates Director at the northern-based brewery, he made it plain that there was no plan to brew again at Foxearth because it would be 'uneconomic' to do so.

He wrote about the meeting in a private aide memoir:

"I was expecting a rather 'high pressure' and difficult meeting with Carfoot concerning the sale of Ward & Son Ltd, but on the contrary the conversation was most formal and extremely friendly. He commenced by going through my letter which I had written to him, and said he quite understood my motives for wishing to buy back the business. I hinted that I thought it would be most uneconomic for me to consider brewing again at Foxearth and therefore did not really want to buy the brewery block of buildings, but of course would be willing to do so if they considered a package deal the simplest way of

dealing with the matter. He then asked me if I did not intend brewing whether I would be prepared to buy beer from Ind Coope for supply to my [licensed] houses. To this I replied that he must realise that if my venture was to succeed, I must be entirely free to buy my beer from whomsoever I wished. He replied that he could entirely see my point of view and presumed that I wanted my [licensed] houses to be virtually free houses.

"He informed me that Ward and Son Ltd would cease to exist as a company from 2 November 1959 as it was to be incorporated into their trading company Ind Coope (East Anglia) Ltd, and at this I expressed concern, pointing out that I felt reasonably confident that my family's name still meant something in East Anglia to many people. It seemed to have the desired effect and Carfoot hastily added that he felt sure I could form a new company using the old name, even if it meant Ind Coope allowing this to be done under licence !

"Finally Carfoot said that any employees that I decided were redundant, would benefit under the Ind Coope scheme for redundant personnel. This I sensed was nearing the last and final round. I purposely avoided mentioning any compensation for loss of office regarding myself as I did not want to antagonise him in any way at this stage and he did not raise the matter either.

"My definite impression is that the bait has been well laid and there is a good likelihood of the fish taking."

His superb optimism was not misplaced and estimations of a buy out seemed higher than ever. Due to rationalisation, Ind Coope had been contemplating selling off some of Taylor Walker's smaller acquisitions, convincing itself that the Foxearth site came into this category. At first Ind Coope management placed a value of £100,000 on the entire estate though skilful negotiating by David's accountants dropped the price sharply within a month.

Ind Coope had been determined to get more for the Estate than they had paid for it, now they realised that this was going to be an impossible fulfilment. Their total consideration was David Ward would buy back all that Taylor Walker had bought for £82,200. David for his part refused, saying he would not go above £70,000.

On 18 October 1959, after a meeting with his advisers, David Ward wrote to Carfoot, suggesting his wanted limitations of responsibility:

As you know, the business has been in my family now for three generations and I and my family feel very loathe to think that it should terminate and the name be lost. For this reason, and whilst I fully appreciate how difficult it will be for me to make a success of the job, I would like to have another try, and I feel that in one way or another, and perhaps with the help of the mineral water side, I shall be able to keep it going.

The cottage property and the brewery would present a problem to me and I would prefer not to have them. However, if you feel that I must take everything that was in the original sale then so be it. In my previous offer to you I tried to be as generous as possible, because I do want my old business back again, but there is a limit beyond which I am advised I should be taking too big a risk.

On the basis of the Trading & Profit Loss Accounts for the period ended 29th August 1959, I must face a possible loss of at least £7,000 between the 1st January and the 30th June 1960, and this sum together with the cost of stocks, possibly book debts and credits for empties, may well take the amount of capital required over £100,000. This is too big a sum of money for me to risk on this venture."

The negotiations continued until January 1960, by which time David had improved his offer to £75,000 for 26 licensed premises; all fixed and current assets and share capital. Later that month he was told his bid would be recommended to the Ind Coope Board of Subsidiary Committees for acceptance.

By first selling the business of Ward and Company Limited, and then buying the drastically re-modelled business back again, he had created a precedent in the brewing industry, the firm assumed a new identity and traded as Wards (Foxearth) Limited. David was upbeat now that the short interlude of Ind Coope tenure was over.

Yet, there was an equivocation in the rather muscular agreement, the brewing giant building in a number of strict conditions. All Ward's pubs, although free houses, were required to sell Ind Coope beers such as Double Diamond, Skol and Long Life.

Other beers such as Jubilee Stout together with beers from Tolly Cobbald, Adnams, Elgoods, Steward and Pattison and Morgans of Norwich were also sold, as was Carling Black Label from the Hope and Anchor Brewery in Sheffield.

Although a reciprocal trading arrangement helped to justify feelings of optimism - Ward's were to supply mineral waters and soft drinks to all Ind Coope pubs within a radius of 17 miles from Foxearth – this incurred a ten per cent royalty on all sales.

Inside twelve months the main brewhouse tower was demolished along with many of the other buildings including the engine sheds and the chimney stack. The fermenting vessels, coppers and other useable equipment were bought by Britain's oldest brewer Shepherd Neame located at Faversham in Kent.[39] Other brewery plant including the 1904 Lancashire boiler and the smaller original Cornish boiler were sold for scrap to make space for the extensive bottling hall.

For the first time in four years, the brewery was again under Ward ownership; well equipped to meet a demanding future. Now head of his own firm, David's hectic business life often melted into his equally demanding social life. For some years he had been a leading light of the local Licensed Victuallers Association (LVA) and at one of these meetings he met a representative of the specialist beer and lager brewers, the Hope & Anchor Brewery at Sheffield - part of the vast Charrington United Breweries group.

In July 1963, during a convivial meeting at Hunter's Lodge, Charrington's chairman E.P. 'Eddie' Taylor, formerly of Canadian Breweries and the man largely responsible for introducing Carling Black Label into the UK, talked to David about selling his business interests. Taylor had not yet secured an unassailable lead for lager in the UK market and his company still needed to reform drinking tastes, which he could only do with the help of the tied trade.

David, hoping to avoid charges of precocity, said he would give thought to the kind of offer which he felt he should obtain; feeling confident that any new ideas for the company should be auspicious

---

[39] The copper is still in use today and is used to brew beers such as Bishop's Finger and Spitfire.

to both his workforce and the Ward name. Finally succumbing to his father's views, perhaps, and taking as vindication the fact that ending the family's ownership of the brewery was a blow to his workforce's morale, he made sure that Charrington's committed themselves to employing all existing staff and keep Ward's (Foxearth) Limited as a nominal member of the huge group - a significant and symbolic role. In a series of moves begun that summer and finalised by that wintry Christmas, the Ward family finally ended its latterly fragmented devotion to brewing.

The final deal saw the brewery run as a local depot supplying London beers to public houses branded as Wards but resigned as Charrington's, and as promised the trading company was still titled Wards (Foxearth) Limited.

As well as being the depot manager, David was rewarded with a directorship of the Dunmow Brewery and was Other Brewers Director of Charrington's's (East Anglia Division). The company was in no hurry to make pronouncements and the deal was kept quiet until the following May when the *Suffolk Free Press* splashed the news:

The directors of Wards (Foxearth) Ltd, brewers and wine and spirit merchants, announced last week that their company had been sold by private treaty to Charrington United Breweries.

Wards managing director Mr D.H. Ward, said his company had no further comment to make on this.

In London last week, Galigzine and Partners, who deal with Charrington's press and publicity material, said that Charrington's's had owned Wards for some little time. They had no statement to make apart from saying that there were no definite plans for the Essex concern at the moment.

Properties belonging to the Wards include the Four Swans Hotel, Sudbury. Charrington United Breweries Ltd who came into being in 1962, brought about the merger of two large brewery groups - Charrington & Company Ltd and United Breweries Ltd.

Charrington & Company Ltd has been brewing at the Anchor Brewery, Mile End, London since 1757. It has expanded very considerably in recent years and at the time of the merger with

United Breweries owned over 2,400 licensed premises in the South of England.

The group now owns altogether 4,900 on-licensed premises and 655 off-licences. It has 10,000 employees, excluding those in the retail establishments.

Over the next decade Charrington merged with Bass, to become Bass Charrington - Britain's biggest brewer. David Ward continued with his new career until his retirement in 1981. In 1987, Harold died aged 89 on the very day in March that the Foxearth depot closed for good.

In the years after his retirement David was able to concentrate on enjoying the tranquillity of Foxearth, endorsed by the memories of his family's glorious past, until he too died in September 1997.

There is little to see of the business that once gave a dependent living to so many people down the years. The office buildings and the Engine House (now called the Pump House) remain, but the great buildings were demolished a generation ago and a housing estate, known as The Chase, built in their place.

With the wisdom of hindsight, it may look that the directors of the brewery acted hastily when it was sold and nearly half a century since its closure, people still lament its death. At the time of its sale, the firm was doing relatively well and making the right products at the right time, which in the past had carried the Ward's to fame and prosperity. Rather than merely making money, they were interested in making better products and building them up to a heady standard, not down to a price.

But perhaps it was this virtue that led the sell out. In the past, farsighted investment had been the bulwark which had allowed the company to overtake the competition by every measurable yardstick of achievement. But in the 1950s, capital for research and development was in short supply, so it must have seemed a prudent economy to accept the Taylor Walker deal. Irresolution over the popularity of beer and the fashion for lager, may also have influenced the decision to sell.

The brewery was many things to many people, but now we are left only with the essential aspect of its inescapable and marvellous legacy. It was right to put away the sunlit past before success became elusive.

Plenty of beer but no brewery. The Foxearth depot 1978

CHRONOLOGY

Brief Chronology of the brewery and Ward's of Foxearth

1814	George Ward born at Foxearth
1824	Charlotte Miller born at Walsham Le Willows, Suffolk
1848	George Ward begins brewing beer at Foxearth thought to be at Mill in Mill Lane
1851	George Ward marries Charlotte Miller at SS Peter & Paul, Foxearth
1855	The Lion Beer house occupied by George and Charlotte Ward to brew and sell beer
1859	David Ward born at Foxearth
1878	George Ward dies aged 64. Charlotte Ward begins trading as Charlotte Ward & Son
1880	David joins his mother as brewer on his 21st birthday.
1880	First purpose brewery is built
1885	George Anthony Foster dies
1886	First bottling line is installed
1888	First large scale brewery is built on land owned by Rev John Foster
1889	Land first leased to David Ward by Rev John Foster
1899	The Lion Beerhouse gains its own licence and becomes The Lion public house
1891	Artesian wells bored at brewery
1891	George Bernard Ward born at Foxearth
1892	Rev John Foster dies aged 79
1893	Foxearth Mineral Water Company opens for business
1894	Brewery and land to be sold at auction. David Ward buys various lots by private treaty
1897	Three-storied brew house block built in the year of Queen Victoria's Golden Jubilee

1897	David Ward becomes first company chairman after Charlotte Ward retires from the business
1898	Harold Ewart Ward born at Foxearth. Company called Ward & Son's
1902	Charlotte Ward dies aged 78
1912	Foxearth beer advertised as 'The National Beverage'
1912	Final major extensions completed
1914	Electricity supplied from brewery to village reading room
1914	Opening of Men's Club. Rev K Foster offered cow- byre (in Love Lane) for first meeting.
1917	George Bernard Ward is killed in the Great War aged 26. He is awarded a bar to his Military Cross
1919	Becomes a public limited company offering 40,000 shares at £1 each. Trades as Ward & Son Ltd
1920	Acquisition of rival brewer Frederick Grice of Cock & Bell, Melford
1931	Celebration of 50 years of 1881 brewery
1943	G.E. Cook of Halstead make offer for brewery. Offer is declined
1949	David Ward dies aged 90 and Harold Ward becomes the firm's second chairman
1949	Tollemarche make offer for brewery. Offer is declined
1957	Cockburns make offer for Brewery. Offer is declined
1957	Taylor Walker & Co buys the brewery and estate including 31 tied houses and off licenses
1958	Last brew of 62 barrels of Small Best Bitter Ale made by David H Ward on 19 February
1960	David H.Ward buys back business (delivery depot and pubs) for £75,000.
1960	Company now titled Wards (Foxearth) Limited
1960	Brewery cleared to allow space for storage and bottling
1961	Demolition of main brew house tower and other out-buildings

1962	Mineral Water business is closed down
1963	Wards (Foxearth) Limited sold to Charrington United Breweries. D.H. Ward continues as manager
1975	Village Club (supported by Wards) closes due to lack of funds
1980	David H. Ward retires
1982	Harold Ewart Ward dies aged 89
1988	Brewery site is sold for £250,000
1989	Final demolition of brewery site except engine house and office
1990s	Site redeveloped for residential use and now known as The Chase
1997	David H. Ward dies aged
2003	Kendrick Foster (great nephew of John Foster and last of Foster line) dies at Lustleigh, Devon
2004	Brewing of a Foxearth beer by Nethergate Brewery, Clare, Suffolk, based on one of the original recipes used by Ward & Sons (circa 1910) Beer named Foxearth 1910

APPENDIX

Facts and figures

Head Brewers (known)

George Ward
Charlotte Ward
David Ward
James Cutmore
Charles Thomson
Junius Charles Ritchie
W H A Barnes
Thomas Fuller (serving pupilage from Fuller's Brewery, Bedford)
Harold Bailey (serving pupillage from Bailey & Tebbuts, Panton Brewery, Cambridge)
Martin Bailey (serving pupillage from Bailey & Tebbuts, Panton Brewery, Cambridge
Bernard Ward (assistant brewer)
Charles Maxim
Fred Carter
Mr Carpenter
Mr Parmenter
Mr Richards
Harold Ward
Mr Trethowan
Martin Falwasser
J.A. (Ned) Middleton
David H Ward

Houses where the Wards lived

Lion Beerhouse
The Brewery House
The Cottage (Foxearth Lodge)
Lower Hall
Carbonell's Farm
Brick cottages opposite the school in Foxearth
Sunny Side (now Magnolia House)

Barrels of beer brewed in 1955 and 1956 (last two years as an independent brewery)

1955 5,307
1956 4,650

Number of bottles produced during two years as an independent brewery

1955 33,792
1956 31,044

Minerals manufactured in 1956

Minerals - dozen bottles half pints and splits -...................... 23,229
Magnums - dozen bottles 4,571
Siphons 1,173
Cordials 7,381

The Ward family and their children - from 1814

Samuel and Martha -	George, Haviot, Amelia (died by drowning, aged 3) Mary, Samuel,
George and Charlotte -	Amelia, David, George Ward Miller, adopted by Charlotte in 1878
David Ward and Louisa -	Gertrude, Winifred, Madge, Harold and George Bernard
Harold and Mary -	Barbara, David, Elizabeth
David H Ward and Marie -	Louise
Louise and Nicholas -	Julia, Candida and Henry

Suppliers

Malt   After the mid-1880s malt was supplied by various firms including varieties from: R & A Allen; Branwhite's at Long Melford; Alfred Gough of Saffron Walden; I. Gough of Bury St Edmunds; EDME Ltd; Fison's; Mackeson; Thompson's; Pidcocks (Nottingham); R & W Paul Ipswich; Ipswich Malting Company; Harrington's of Ware in Hertfordshire. Latterly it came from Gilstrap, Earl and Company of Newark and James Hole and Company's brewery also in Newark. Oat malt was supplied by Brooks & Son. Early suppliers of malt included Alf Thompson at Borley; William (and then Frederick) Ince at Mill Lane, Foxearth and John Butcher at Bulmer.

Hops   Hop merchants (mostly based in Kent and Sussex) included: Arthur Morris; E Clemens Horst (London); Henry Barrett; Wood, Fielding and Horbury; Tabrum & Son; Baker White & Morgan; Arthur Walton; Young and Company; Preston Son & Elliot; Webb & Son. Glaziers, Sussex.

Yeast   Wandsworth Brewery supplied various yeast including: 30 XX, No 3 and No 7 The British Pure Yeast Co supplied their eponymous brand - British Pure Yeast. Cannon's Brewery supplied 67 KK and 77 KK plus many others including Shipton Yeast Co who marketed Shipton's Slow Yeast and Marston's who marketed Birmingham Yeast and Marston's Yeast. Greene King also supplied yeast immediately after the 1914-1918 War.

Sugar   Various sugars were supplied by: Clark & Son (caramel, black syrup) Boake Roberts (Caramel, inverted glucose, corpulose) Kendall & Son (New Copper Sugar and Invert Laevuline); Paisley Sugar Company (caramelised diastase syrup, septose, raw sugar.) Gonville & Jarvis (caramel, raw sugar) Gartons (invert glucose and diastase syrup) Buttsons (caramel) J.M Collett & Co (Special Stout Sugar, malt extract) Sugar & Malt Products Ltd (raw and cooked sugars) Barrett, Tagant and Gotts (invert sugar)

Syrups and essence suppliers (for soft drinks) included: Duckworth's of Lancashire; Stevens & Howell; Bush; Barnett & Foster.

Hop varieties used included :

Poperinghe, Pacific; Oregon Setts; Buss, Hoad, Marzill Goldings; Saaz; Sanomas; Williams Choice; Cradduck; Choice Farnham; Le Feave; Coppins; Hughes K; Pudge; Homewood; Stears; Lord; Holmes; Davis; Baker; Vane; Holledaw; Waulzach; Wigan; Readers; Nicholls; Kapells; Keysells; Burgess; Palma; Caliph; Bugg; Alsace; Plumptree; Elsam Sussex; Boddington; Moat Farm; Scotts; Repacks.

List of medals and dates (few dates can be traced)

1908 - Brewery wins first prize and Silver Medal at the Brewer's Exhibition for Pale Ale

1910 - First prize and silver medal for bottled pale ale: second prizes for oatmeal stout and pale ale in cask

1911 - Second British brewery to win Grand Prix and Gold Medal at Paris International Expot.

1913 - Brewery wins Gold Medal at the Brewers Exhibition for Imperial Pale Ale in cask

1925 - Brewery wins Silver Medal for bottled strong ale

1936 - Brewery wins Gold Medal at the Brewers Exhibition for Imperial Pale Ale

1952 - Brewery wins first prize for bottled stout at the National Brewers Exhibition at Olympia

Brewery staff who attended David Ward's funeral (1949)

Messrs A.D Gray, W. Coe, J.A. Middleton, H.A. Sewell, H. Brockwell, Mr K Coleby, Miss C Bloor, Miss V Grant, Mrs W.J. Sutton, Mrs V. Inch, Mrs E Mansfield, Mrs Coleby; T Chinery, F. Chinery; Jas Carter, H.J. Mills, H.S. Mills, V. Inch, F. Inch; H. Byham, F. Bareham, A Farrance, P. Gridley; R.J. Newman, E. Mansfield; J. Macauley, H.A Ford, G.C Ford, H. Parmenter; R.J. Parcheut; P.W Chatters; Henry Cook; C. Arbon, T. Read; W.J. Sutton; S. Steggles, C.J Cutmore; G. Mingay; A Watson; R.G Gammon; J. Duce; E.A. Heathcoate.

Range of beers

In bottles *(original gravity (o.g.) where known)*
Imperial Ale .... (o.g 1046)
No. 1 Strong Ale .... (o.g. 1080)
Imperial Double Brown .... (o.g. 1044)
Nourishing Stout .... (1045)
Oatmeal Stout .... (1048)
Burton Ale .... (1038)
Gold Medal Pale Ale .... (1039)
Small Best Bitter Ale .... (o.g. 1031)
Coronation Ale (1911) .... (o.g. 1004)
Light Tonic Ale .... (1033)

On draught

Draught XXXX .... (1046) Strong stock ale
XX Rich Mild Ale .... (o.g. 1027)
BA .... (1035) - best ale
SBB .... (1033) - small best beer
BBA .... (o.g. 1039) - best bitter ale
X1 .... Special Dinner Ale
IPA .... (1033) - Imperial Pale Ale
KK .... Medium Bitter
AK .... Light Tonic Bitter

Public houses owned by the firm (in all of its guises)

The Bear Inn (Sudbury)
Cock and Bell (Long Melford)
Great Eastern Hotel (Sudbury)
Prince of Wales (Sudbury)
Green Dragon (Sudbury)
The Cock (Clare)
Four Swans (Sudbury)
The Swan (Little Waldingfield)
The Eagle (Welnetham)
The Bull (Cavendish)
Black Fox (Thurston)
Royal Oak (Bradley, Nr Stradishall)
Queens Arms (Great Cornard)
Queens Head Hotel (Haverhill)
The Ram (Hadleigh)
Four Swans (Sudbury)
Eight Bells (Belchamp Walter)
Red Lion (Belchamp Otten)
Cherry Tree Inn (Knowl Green)
Plough Inn (Bulmer)
Cock and Blackbird (Bulmer)
Red Cow (Sudbury)
Cherry Tree (Glemsford)
The Green Man (Belchamp St Paul)
Hare and Hounds (Sudbury)
The Crown - Glemsford

The Pinkuah Arms (Pentlow) [40]

Bar prices at the Foxearth Men's Club on its closure in 1975

Abbot Ale	16p for half pint bottle;
Shandy	25p per pint;
Guinness	17.5p for half pint bottle;
Light Ale (Toby or Adnams)	28p per pint or 14d for half;
Tolly dark or Harvest	28p a pint;
Mackeson	15p;
Double Diamond	18p;
Lucozade (small)	15p;
26oz lemonade	15p;
cider	13p;
bitter lemon, tonic water, ginger ale,	9p
Bottle deposits - minerals	5p
all others.	3p
Coca Cola	12p;
Minster Lemonade	35p;
Gin/Rum/Whisky	25p per tot.
Minatures	41p.
Half bottles of Gin/Rum/Whisky	£2.36.
Bottles	£4.63.
quarter bottles of spirits	£1.21

Composition of water used for brewing – *high degree of organic purity*

	(grains per gallon)
Ammonia free and saline	0.0126
Ammonia albuminoidal	0.0045
Oxygen absorbed in 1 hour	0.98

---

[40] This pub did not receive a full on-licence until 1929. It was bought off the Bull family in 1928 and owned for just under 12 months. Ward's bored a well on the site but for reasons unknown.

Oxygen absorbed in 3 hours	0.103
Nitrogen as nitrates	very slight trace
Nitrogen as nitrites	none
Chlorine	5.7
Total solid residue dried at 180°	35.8
Carbonic anhydride CO_2	9.13
Suphuric anhydride SO_3	2.50
Lime CaO	9.91
Manganese MGo	2.44
Potash K_2O	
Silica	1.26
Oxides of iron and aluminium	0.28
Alkalinity before boiling as CaO	20.72
Alkalinity after boiling as calcium carbonate	4.37
Ph value	7.46

Summary of barrels brewed in 1908/1909 – only surviving record of early production

Quality	1908 Barrels	1909 Barrels	Increase	Decrease
XXXX	582 ¾	479 ½	103 ½	
BA	503 ¾	434 ¾	69	
"Quilter"	nil	254 ¼	254 ¼	
KK	5,574 ¾	6028 ½	453 ¾	
AK	711 ½	670 ¾		40 ¾
XX	741 ¼	504 ½		236 ¾
XI	1,552 ¼	1,547		5 ¼
Stout	2, 545	2, 546 ¾	1 ¾	
Porter	nil	224	224	
Cheap	159 ½	105 ¾		53 ¾
TOTAL	12,370 ¾	12,795 ¾	933 ¾	508 ¾
Beer duty	£4442.6.0	£4577. 10. 9	£135. 4. 9	
			425 barrels increase	

Beer Sales in 1955/1956

(last year as an independent family-owned brewery)

Products	1955	1956	Average price in £ S D - 1955	Average price £ S D in 1956
All beers	4,843	4,508	16.12.1	16.14.2
Cask beers	1,927	1,861	13.15.9	13.13.6
Bottles Bottled beers	2,916	2,916	18.09.1 (per dozen	18.16.10 (per dozen)

Glossary of Beer and Brewing Terms

Acetaldehyde   Green apple aroma, a by-product of fermentation.

Additive   Enzymes, preservatives and antioxidants which are added to simplify the brewing process or prolong shelf life.

Adjunct   Fermentable material used as a substitute for traditional grains, to make beer lighter-bodied or cheaper.

Aerobic   An organism, such as top fermenting ale yeast, that needs oxygen to metabolise.

Alcohol   Ethyl alcohol or ethanol. An intoxicating by-product of fermentation, caused by yeast acting on sugars in the malt. Alcohol content is expressed as a percentage of volume or weight.

Alcohol   An intoxicating by-product of fermentation, which is caused by yeast acting on the sugars in the malt.

Alcohol by volume   Amount of alcohol in beer in terms of percentage volume of alcohol per volume of beer.

Alcohol by weight   Amount of alcohol in beer measured in terms of the percentage weight of alcohol per volume of beer, i.e., 3.2% alcohol by weights equals

3.2 grams of alcohol per 100 centilitres of beer. (It is approximately 20% less than alcohol by volume.)

Alcoholic   Warming taste of ethanol and higher alcohol's.

Ale   Beers distinguished by use of top fermenting yeast strains, Saccharomyces cerevisiae. The top fermenting yeast perform at warmer temperatures than do yeast's used to brew lager beer, and their by-products are more evident in taste and aroma. Fruitiness and esters are often part of ale's character.

Ale   One of the larger families of beers. True ales are fermented with top-fermenting yeast. They are low in carbonation and served warm.

Amber   Any top or bottom fermented beer having an amber colour, that is, between pale and dark.

Amylase   Enzymes that liquefy starches and convert them to maltose (sugar) and dextrin's.

Anaerobic   An organism, such as a bottom-fermenting lager yeast, that is able to metabolise without oxygen present.

Aroma   The particular combination of smells from malt, hops, yeast, and any unusual or distinctive disturbances in the beer.

Aroma Hops   Varieties of hop chosen to impart bouquet. (See Hops) Astringent A drying, puckering taste; tannic; can be derived from boiling the grains, long mashes, over sparging or sparging with hard water.

Attenuation   Extent to which yeast consumes fermentable sugars (converting them into alcohol and carbon dioxide).

Bacterial   A general term covering off-flavours such as mouldy, musty, woody, lactic acid, vinegar, or microbiological spoilage.

Balance   Hoppiness versus maltiness -The complexity of

	interaction, and a measure of the brewer's skill.
Barley	A cereal grain malted for use in the grist that becomes the mash in the brewing of beer.
Barrel	A unit of measurement. A barrel holds 36 imperial gallons (1 imperial gallon = 4.5 litres),
Beer	Name given to alcohol-containing beverages produced by fermenting grain, specifically malt, and flavoured with hops. Introduced into Britain by the Saxons and Danes.
Beer Styles	The three major beer styles are lagers, ales, and specialty beers. Specialty beers are brewed with various non-standard ingredients.
Beer	A fermented beverage made from barley. hops, water, and yeast, and sometimes other ingredients.
Bitter	Bitterness of hops or malt husks; sensation on back of tongue.
Bitterness	The perception of a bitter flavour, in beer from iso-alpha-acid in solution (derived from hops). It is measured in International Bitterness Units (IBU).
Bitterness-	The taste component added by hops.
Black malt	Partially malted barley roasted at high temperatures. Black malt gives a dark colour and roasted flavour to beer.
Black Patent Malt	Malted barley roasted at high temperatures to give colour and taste to the beer.
Body	The particular feel of a beer is described as full-bodied, medium-bodied, or light bodied, depending on the sense of thickness or thinness in your mouth.
Body	Thickness and mouth-filling property of a beer described as "full or thin bodied".
Bottle conditioning	Secondary fermentation and maturation in the bottle, creating complex aromas and flavours.
Bottle of Beer	A bottle of beer equals twelve fluid ounces.

Bottom-fermenting yeast	One of the two types of yeast used in brewing. Bottom-fermenting yeast works well at low temperatures and ferments more sugars leaving a crisp, clean taste and then settles to the bottom of the tank. Also referred to as "lager yeast".
Bottom-fermenting Yeast (Lager Yeast)	The yeast used to ferment lagers. This yeast works at colder temperatures than ale yeast and settles to the bottom of the fermentation vessel.
Brew house	The collective equipment used to make beer.
Bright Beer Tank	See conditioning tank.
Bung	The stopper in the hole in a keg or cask through which the keg or cask is filled and emptied. The hole may also be referred to as a bung or bunghole. Real beer must use a wooden bung.
Butterscotch	See diacetyl.
Cabbage like	Aroma and taste of cooked vegetables; often a result of wort spoilage bacteria killed by alcohol in fermentation.
CAMRA	The CAMpaign for Real Ale. An organization founded in 1971 to preserve the production of cask-conditioned beers and ales.
Carbonation	Sparkle caused by carbon dioxide, either created during fermentation or injected later.
Carbon Dioxide (CO2)	A gas consisting of one part carbon and two parts oxygen released during fermentation.
Caramel	A cooked sugar used to add colour and alcohol content to beer. It is often used in place of more expensive malted barley.
Caramel malt	sweet, coppery-coloured malt. Caramel or crystal malt imparts both colour and flavour to beer. Caramel malt has a high concentration of unfermentable sugars that sweeten the beer and, contribute to head retention. Also known as crystal malt.

Cask	A closed, barrel-shaped container for beer. They come in various sizes and are now usually made of metal. The bung in a cask of "Real" beer or ale must be made of wood to allow the pressure to be relieved, as the fermentation of the beer, in the cask, continues.
Cask conditioning	Secondary fermentation and maturation in the cask at the point of sale. Creates light carbonation.
Chlorophenolic	A plastic-like aroma; caused by chemical combination of chlorine and organic compounds.
Chill haze	Cloudiness caused by precipitation of protein-tannin compound at low temperatures, does not affect flavour.
Chill Haze	A condition occurring in some beers at low (near freezing) temperatures caused by proteins in the beer becoming cloudy. Not an indication of bad beer.
Chill proof	Beer treated to allow it to withstand cold temperatures without clouding.
Clove-like	Spicy character reminiscent of cloves; characteristic of some wheat beers, or if excessive, may derive from wild yeast.
Conditioning	Period of maturation intended to impart "condition"(natural carbonation). Warm conditioning further develops the complex of flavours. Cold conditioning imparts a clean, round taste.
Conditioning Tank	A vessel, in which beer is placed after primary fermentation where the beer matures, clarifies and, is naturally carbonated through secondary fermentation. Also called bright beer tank, serving tank and, secondary tank.
Conditioning	The process of creating carbonation in the finished beer, typically taking place in the bottle or keg after sugar is added. Conditioning

can also mean aging or laagering beer.

Contract Brewing	Making beer for smaller companies that either do not have a brewery of their own or lack the capacity to meet demand.
Contract Beer	Beer made by one brewery and then marketed by a company calling itself a brewery. The latter uses the brewing facilities of the former.
Copper	The vessel in which wort from the mash is boiled with hops. Also sometimes called a brew kettle.
Decoction	Exhaustive system of mashing in which portions of the wort are removed, heated, then returned to the original vessel.
Dextrin	The un-fermentable carbohydrate produced by the enzymes in barley. It gives the beer flavour, body, and mouth-feel. Lower temperatures produce more dextrin and less sugar. While higher temperatures produce more sugars and less dextrin.
Dextrins	Non (or slowly) fermentable carbohydrates found in the malt. They give beer flavour, body, and mouth-feel.
Diacetyl	A volatile compound in beer that contributes to a butterscotch flavour, measured in parts per million.
DMS	Taste and aroma of sweet corn; results from malt, as a result of the short or weak boil of the wort, slow wort chilling, or bacterial infection.
Dimethyl sulphide	a sulphur compound.
Dosage	The addition of yeast and/or sugar to the cask or bottle to aid secondary fermentation.
Draft (Draught)	The process of dispensing beer from a bright tank, cask or, keg, by hand pump, pressure from an air pump or, injected carbon dioxide inserted into the beer container prior to sealing.

Dry-hopping	The addition of dry hops to fermenting or aging beer to increase its hop character or aroma.
EBC	European Brewing Convention. An EBC scale is used to indicate colours in malts and beers.
Enzymes	Catalysts found naturally in the grain. When heated in mash, they convert the starches of the malted barley into maltose, a sugar used in solution and fermented to make beer.
Ester	Volatile flavour compound naturally created in fermentation. Often fruity, flowery or spicy.
Esters	Esters are organic compounds that result from the interaction of acids and alcohol. The presence of esters can cause the fruity flavours and aromas, such as banana, blueberry, and pear, that intentionally or unintentionally occur in some beers.
Estery	Aroma or flavour reminiscent of flowers or fruits.
Fahrenheit (degrees)	$F = (C \times 9) (5) + 32.$
Fermentation	This is the process of producing alcohol and carbon dioxide through the actions of yeast on grain-based sugars.
Fermentation	Conversion of sugars into ethyl alcohol and carbon dioxide, through the action of yeast.
Final specific gravity	Specific gravity of a beer when fermentation is complete (that is, all fermentable sugars have been fermented).
Fining	A process of producing a bright beer by clearing the beer of unwanted haze or yeast, by adding ingredients such as isinglass or gelatine.
Fining	An aid to clarification: a substance that attracts particles that would otherwise remain suspended in the brew.
Filter	The removal of designated impurities by

passing the wort through a medium, sometimes made of diatomaceous earth (made up of the microscopic skeletal remains of marine animals). Yeast in suspension is often targeted for removal.

Filtering	The process of passing beer through a porous substance to clarify it. This process occurs after fermentation.
Grains	(such as rice, corn, maize, or wheat) used in addition to malted barley to make a beer. They tend to lighten the flavour of a beer and produce alcohol.
Grainy	Tastes like cereal or raw grain.
Gravity (Specific)	The weight of a liquid relative to the weight of an equal volume of water. Specific gravity must be checked before and after fermentation. Used as an indication of the amount of alcohol present in the finished beer.
Grist	Brewers' term for milled grains, or the combination of milled grains to be used in a particular brew. Derives from the verb to grind. Also sometimes applied to hops.
Grist	Dry mixture of barley malts and adjuncts used in mashing.
Hang	Lingering bitterness or harshness.
Head	Foam that forms on top of the beer when it is poured. Head tends to indicate the degree of carbonation, hops, and malt in the beer.
Heat Exchanger	A mechanical device used to rapidly reduce the temperature of the wort.
Hogshead	Cask holding 54 imperial gallons (243 litres).
Hops	One of the four principal ingredients of beer, hops are flower cones added to beer as a bittering agent, a preservative, and an aromatic.
Hop back	Sieve-like vessel used to strain out the petals of the hop flowers.

Hops	Herb added to boiling wort or fermenting beer to impart a bitter aroma and flavour.
Hoppy	Aroma of hops, does not include hop bitterness.
Hydrometer	A thermometer-like device used to measure the specific gravity to determine the proportion of potential alcohol in the beer.
IBU	International Bitterness units. A system of indicating the hop bitterness in finished beer.
Infusion	Simplest form of mash, in which grains are soaked in water. May be at a single temperature, or with upward or (occasionally) downward changes.
Infusion	The process of introducing mash into hot water for mashing. The infusion method of mashing involves mashing a single time at a constant temperature, as opposed to other, more complex mashing techniques that involve mashing more than once at different heat levels.
Isinglass	Material made from fish bladders used to clarify beer (finings).
Irish Moss	A seaweed that is added to boiling wort to filter proteins.
Keg	One-half barrel equalling 18 gallons
Lager	From the German word to store, lagers represent a major family of beers. They have a longer and cooler fermentation period than ales, and are brewed with bottom-fermenting yeast.
Lagering	Aging the beer by letting it stand for a number of days in a lagering tank.
Lagering	From the German word for storage. Refers to maturation for several weeks or months at cold temperatures (close to 0°C /32°F) to settle residual yeast, impart carbonation and make

	for clean round flavours.
Lambic	Spontaneously fermented wheat beers from Belgium. The yeast is not manually added; instead, it is allowed to drift in from the surrounding countryside.
Length	The amount of wort brewed each time the brew house is in operation.
Light-struck	Beer damaged by exposure to light. Also known as corona.
Light-Struck	Skunk like smell; from exposure to light.
Liquor	The water used in making beer.
Liquor	The brewer's word for water used in the brewing process, as included in the mash or, used to sparge the grains after mashing.
Malt (ing)	The process by which barley is steeped in water, germinated ,then kilned to convert insoluble starch to soluble substances and sugar. The foundation ingredient of beer.
Malt Extract	The condensed wort from a mash, consisting of maltose, dextrins and, other dissolved solids. Either as a syrup or powdered sugar, it is used by brewers, in solutions of water and extract, to reconstitute wort for fermentation.
Malt Extract	Syrups manufactured by evaporating excess water out of wort
Malted Barley	The basis of beer. Malted barley is created by germinating barley for optimum starch content and enzyme development, then drying it quickly. This provides starches that convert to sugars, which then ferment into alcohol and CO_2.
Maltose	The main fermentable sugar obtained from malted grains.
Mash	(Verb) To release malt sugars by soaking the grains in water. (Noun) The resultant mixture.
Mash Tun	The double-jacketed, stainless-steel vessel in

which mashing occurs.

Mash Tun
A tank where grist is soaked in water and heated in order to convert the starch to sugar and extract the sugars and other solubles from the grist.

Mashing
The preparation of the wort, the liquid base of beer. Mashing converts starches to sugars by mixing malted barley with hot water.

Maltose
A water soluble, fermentable sugar contained in malt.

Medicinal
Chemical or phenolic character; can be the result of wild yeast, contact with plastic, or sanitizer residue.

Metallic
Tastes tinny, bloodlike or metal-like; may come from bottle caps or metal casks.

Mouth-feel
A sensation derived from the consistency or viscosity of a beer, described, for example as thin or full.

Musty
Mouldy, mildewy character; can be the result of cork or bacterial infection.

Original gravity
A measurement of the density of fermentable sugars in a mixture of malt and water with which a brewer begins a given batch.

Oxidized
Stale - tastes and smells of rotten pineapple, or sherry, as a result of oxygen as the beer ages or is exposed to high temperatures.

Palate
Taste. Influenced by the grains, hops, water, yeast, and adjuncts used in production.

Pale Ale
Light-coloured ales that are usually full-bodied and on the bitter side.

Pasteurisation
Heating of beer to 60-79(°C/140-174°F to stabilize it microbiologically. Flash-pasteurisation is applied very briefly, for 15-60 seconds by heating the beer as it passes through the pipe. Alternately, the bottled beer can be passed on a conveyor belt through a

heated tunnel. This more gradual process takes at least 20 minutes and sometimes much longer.

Pasteurisation The process of heating finished beer to kill all living organisms in it, thereby stabilizing it for shipping and increased shelf life.

Phenolic flavour and aroma of medicine, plastic, smoke, or cloves; caused by wild yeast or bacteria, or sanitizer residue.

Pilsner A type of lager beer, first made in Czechoslovakia in the late 13th century.

Pitch To add yeast to wort.

Pitching Adding yeast to the wort in the fermentation tank.

Plato, degrees Expresses the specific gravity as the weight of extract in a 100 gram solution at 64°F (17.5°C). Refinement of the Balling scale.

Porter A characteristically dark brown beer, of English origin. The bitterness of this beer derives from the use of roasted, un-malted barley.

Priming The addition of sugar at the maturation stage to promote a secondary fermentation.

Primary Fermentation Occurring after pitching the yeast and during the first three days on the average, fermentation converts sugars to alcohol and carbonation. Fermentation time for the microbrewery ranges from three to seven days.

Priming Sugar Sugar added to the bottle or keg that ferments and provides CO_2.

Priming The process of adding sugar to the brew to create carbonation, either in the bottle or keg.

Proteins Nitrogen-containing compounds, an excess of which cause a haze in beer.

Racking The process of separating the fermented beer from the yeast cells at the bottom of the

	fermenting vessel. Also the transfer of finished beer to kegs. Broadly, moving beer from one vessel to another.
Regional specialty brewery	A brewery that produces more than 15,000 barrels of beer annually, with its largest selling product a specialty beer.
Secondary fermentation	Stage of fermentation occurring in a closed container from several weeks to several months.
Sediment	Yeast material at the bottom of the bottle formed as a result of conditioning the beer in the bottle. Not a sign of bad beer.
Shelf life	Describes the number of days a beer will retain it's peak drinkability. The shelf life for commercially produced beers is usually a maximum of four months.
Solvent-like	Reminiscent of acetone or lacquer thinner; caused by high fermentation temperatures.
Sour/Acidic	Vinegar-like or lemon-like; can be caused by bacterial infection.
Specific gravity	A measure of the density of a liquid or solid compared to that of water ((1.000 at 39°F (4°C)).
Sparge	To spray grist with hot water in order to remove soluble sugars (maltose). This takes place at the end of the mash.
Sparging	Rinsing the mashed grains to ensure complete extraction of the sugars from the mash.
Squares	Brewers' term for a square fermenting vessel.
Sweet	Taste like sugar; experienced on the front of the tongue.
Sulphur-like	Reminiscent of rotten eggs or burnt matches; a by-product of some yeast's.
Tart	Taste sensation cause by acidic flavours.
Temporary Hardness	Hardness in water that can be removed by boiling

Terminal gravity	Synonym for final specific gravity.
Top-fermenting yeast	One of the two types of yeast used in brewing. Top-fermenting yeast works better at warmer temperatures and are able to tolerate higher alcohol concentrations than bottom-fermenting yeast. It is unable to ferment some sugars, and results in a fruitier, sweeter beer. Also known as "ale yeast".
Top-Fermenting Yeast (Ale Yeast)	A style of yeast that works at cellar or warm temperatures and floats to the top of the beer. Ale yeasts are responsible for the creation of most beers other than lagers.
Trub	Proteins in barley filtered during the wort boil.
Tun	Any large vessels used in brewing.
Units of bitterness	See IBU.
Vinous	Reminiscent of wine.
Winy	Sherry-like flavour; can be caused by warm fermentation or oxidation in very old beer.
Wort	The solution of grain sugars strained from the mash tun. At this stage, regarded as "sweet wort", later as brewed wort, fermenting wort and finally beer.
Wort	The sweet liquid derived from mashing, or mixing malted barley with water. Wort is the beginning of all beers.
Yeast	A micro-organism of the fungus family. Genus Saccharomyces.
Yeast	Living plant micro-organisms that convert sugars to alcohol and carbon dioxide.
Yeasty	Yeast-like flavour; a result of yeast in suspension or beer sitting too long on sediment.
Zymurgy	The science / art of yeast fermentation.

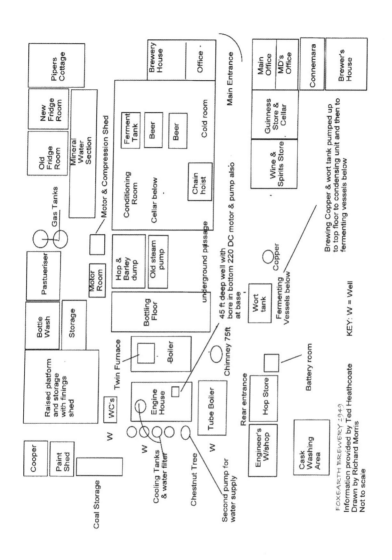

A diagram of the layout of the brewery

PLATES

The splendidly whiskered Rev John Foster in old age

Rev John Foster, Rosalind (left) and Georgina Elizabeth

George Anthony Foster and Henry Marshall c1864

The remarkable David Ward

A Ward & Son dray around 1900

Motorised dray with award winning livery

Hay carting in Ward's meadow c1930s

From a west-facing position with engine house in the foreground

41 Chapel Hill Halstead 1919, the year of its closure

Brewery offices built 1907 on the site of The Lion beerhouse

George Bernard Ward at Lyston Park 1915

Harold Ward, on his retirement

Harold Ward, in his early twenties

ACKNOWLEDGEMENTS

So many people have helped me in so many ways with the compiling and production of this book some with advice and material, others with proof reading - the acknowledgments which I should like to make would take a few hundred words.

But as I have only a limited number of them, I must restrict myself, first to thanking Tom Hastie, for allowing me to have sight of material he has collected over the last twenty years and which forms the nucleus of this book.

Louise Wells generously lent me private material including family letters and photographs. My grateful thanks to Barbara Freeland and Elizabeth & John Harrington; Ashley Cooper, whose valuable assistance made the publication of this book possible; Andrew Clarke for his immense generosity, typesetting skills, occasionally pointing me in the right direction and contacts which include Mark Holborn at Random House; Alan Fitch and the Foxearth District History Society for their boundless enthusiasm for this project; Kate for her patience in reading the first drafts; the Sudbury Mercury and East Anglian Daily Times in the persons of Will Wright and Patrick Lowman for finding me people to speak to and especially Anne Bigelow, Ian Peaty; Carol and Roger Hobbs for allowing me to tap into their resources. Thank you also to Doris Mitchell, Linda Marsh and Jeff Sorrell.

Finally, it would be ungrateful of me to miss this opportunity of thanking a group of ex-Ward's employees including Wilf Braybrooke, Ted Heathcoate and Cliff Arbon for telling me, with much patience, their recollections of times at the brewery. Special thanks to Ian Hornsey and the Nethergate Brewery for brewing a copy beer to celebrate the publication of this book - proving that they are spiritual heirs to the legacy of great East Anglian brewers.

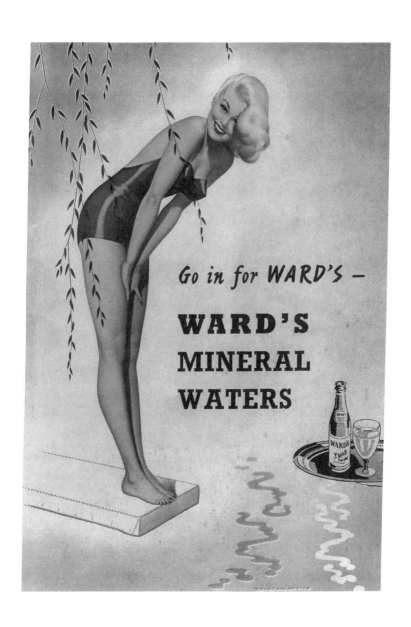

BIBLIOGRAPHY

Ask the Fellows Who Cut The Hay – George Ewart Evans
(published by Faber & Faber)

A History of Beer & Brewing - Ian Hornsey (published by RSC
Paperbacks)

Ward's A Brewing Family by Ian P Peaty (published by the
Brewery History Society. Journal of the Brewery History Society,
Number 100, summer 2000)

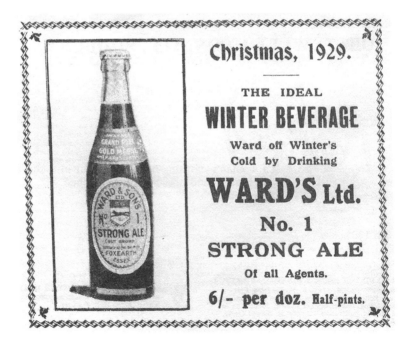

INDEX

ABOUT THE AUTHOR

Richard Morris is a well-known professional journalist who has written widely in the national press, and is a seasoned broadcaster.

Although this is his first book on Local History, Richard has brought to the task many skills and resources learned in the course of researching news stories and has been able to use the unique insights into human nature that come with experience in journalism. Where much of the primary evidence comes from newspaper reports and cuttings, Richard is able to 'read between the lines' and detect where news-management has got the better of integrity.

Above all, Richard knows how to make a story interesting and how to carry the reader along with his enthusiastic pursuit of a fascinating story